THE
GREATEST
TEXTS
OF
THE
BIBLE

Books by Clarence Edward Macartney

Great Women of the Bible
The Greatest Texts of the Bible
Paul the Man

THE
GREATEST
TEXTS
OF THE BIBLE

Clarence E. Macartney

kregel PUBLICATIONS
Grand Rapids, MI 49501

The Greatest Texts of the Bible, by Clarence Edward
Macartney, © 1992 by Kregel Publications, P.O. Box 2607,
Grand Rapids, Michigan 49501. This edition includes mi-
nor changes in the text and arrangement of the sermons.

Cover and Book Design: Alan G. Hartman

Library of Congress Cataloging-in-Publication Data

Macartney, Clarence Edward Noble, 1879-1957.

The Greatest Texts of the Bible / Clarence Edward
Macartney.
        p.   cm.
   Reprint. Originally published: Nashville: Abingdon-
Cokesbury Press, 1947.
   1. Presbyterian Church—Sermons. 2. Sermons,
American. I. Title.
BX9178.M172G69   1992   252'.051—dc20   92-16136
                                                    CIP
ISBN 0-8254-3266-9

        1 2 3 4 5 year / printing 96 95 94 93 92

CONTENTS

PUBLISHER'S PREFACE

For twenty-seven years Dr. Charles Edward Noble Macartney pastored the influential First Presbyterian Church of Pittsburgh, Pennsylvania. Prior to that pastorate he ministered in Paterson, New Jersey, and Philadelphia, Pennsylvania. His preaching especially attracted men, not only to his Sunday services but also to his popular noon luncheons. Because of his skill and eloquence in expounding the lives of Bible characters, he was well-called "the American Alexander Whyte." Still, his preaching was always biblical, doctrinal and practical, albeit topical-textual in approach.

This collection of sermons on the "great texts of the Bible" first appeared in 1947, published by Abingdon-Cokesbury Press. It represents some of his strongest and most impassioned preaching. Except for slight modifications and updating, and the insertion of Scripture references, these sermons are reissued in their original form. It is the publisher's prayer that they will encourage preachers and teachers of today to emphasize these great texts in their preaching and teaching.

FOREWORD

An examination of recent published sermons and of newspaper reports of ministers' subjects reveals that there seems to be a tendency—indeed, a habit—on the part of some preachers today to avoid the great and familiar texts of the Bible, the texts on which successive generations of preachers and believers have rung the changes of praise, wonder, and appeal.

This omission of the great texts of the Bible in the preaching of the day may be due in part to a commendable desire to pass by that which is familiar and oft spoken. But chiefly it is due to an unwillingness to grapple with the truths of divine redemption which the great texts declare. And this in turn is due to the changing emphasis in Christian teaching and preaching, an emphasis which centers upon the ethical and social side of the gospel to the exclusion of the cardinal truths of revelation and redemption.

The great texts frighten the preacher and yet haunt him—too great to preach upon and yet too important to omit. Such are the texts of the sermons in this book. No preacher would dare to say that any small selection of texts he might make contains the *only* great texts in the Bible, but certainly all will agree that among the texts I have chosen for the sermons in this volume are many of the greatest texts of the Bible. When we preach on these texts we are preaching, not to the times, but to the eternities; we are in the company of that angel whom John saw "fly in the midst of heaven, having the everlasting gospel to preach unto them that dwell on the earth" (Rev. 19:17).   CLARENCE EDWARD MACARTNEY

1

YOUR SIN WILL FIND YOU OUT

*Ye have sinned against the Lord: and be sure
your sin will find you out* (Numbers 32:23).

There is only one thing about which you can be absolutely certain. You cannot be sure about the weather, whether blustery March winds will be blowing, or whether the sun will be bright and warm, and the wind soft and balmy with the foretaste of spring. You cannot tell what your material or financial position will be a year from today. You cannot tell where your place of residence will be six months from today. You cannot tell what your state of health will be. You cannot be certain that you will be alive a week from now. Indeed, you cannot be certain that you will die, for Christ may come before you die.

But there is one thing about which you can be sure—"Be sure your sin will find you out." These words were spoken by Moses to the children of Israel. If the people remembered God and kept His commandments, all would be well with them; but if they rebelled against God and turned to follow idols, suffering and retribution would come upon them. The history of Israel shows how true that was. But what was spoken then to a nation is spoken to you and me as individuals—"Be sure your sin will find you out."

A woman had been more sinned against than sinning. Suffering and religious devotion had chastened and purified her character till it was one of rare Christian grace and beauty. She was telling me of a sermon she had heard in Scotland in her childhood on the

9

text, "Be sure your sin will find you out." The divisions of the sermon, as she remembered it after the long lapse of years, were these: in time, in conscience, in eternity. There could be no better arrangement made for a sermon on this text. Let us, therefore, follow these heads and see how sin finds people out, in time, in conscience, and in eternity.

IN TIME

The constitution of the world is moral, and all nature seems to be attuned to the moral law. The proverbs of the nations attest to the universal belief that even in this world sin finds men out in exposure and punishment. We read of some crime that has been committed, and no matter how skillfully it has been perpetrated, and how few the traces and clues as to the guilty person, we are confident that in a few days, a few weeks, or a few months, some-one will be arrested.

This belief in exposure and punishment of guilt finds expression in the exclamation of the barbarians at Malta, when they saw the viper hanging to Paul's arm: "No doubt this man is a murderer, whom, though he hath escaped the sea, yet vengeance suffereth not to live" (Acts 28:4). They were mistaken as to Paul and quickly went to the other extreme and mistook him for a god. But they were not mistaken in their acceptance of the law that evil-doing immediately has punishment and exposure upon its trail.

A French peasant, standing over the body of the murdered Robespierre at the time of the Reign of Terror, exclaimed, looking down upon him: "Yes, Robespierre, there is a God."

The ancients had a saying, "The cranes of Ibicus," by which they expressed their belief in the exposure of sin and evil-doing in time. There is a story behind that saying. A merchant from Corinth was attacked on his journey by a band of robbers, who stripped him and slew him. As he lay dying, the merchant Ibicus appealed to a flock of cranes he saw flying through the heavens to avenge his death. The robbers went to the city of Corinth, and were enjoying themselves at the theater when some cranes flew over head. A half-drunken member of their band, pointing to the cranes, cried out: "There go the cranes of Ibicus."

What he said was overheard by others, and this in time led to the exposure of the crime and the arrest and execution of the robbers. Hence the saying, "The cranes of Ibicus." "Curse not the king, no, not in thy thought," said the wise man, "and curse not the rich in thy bedchamber: for a bird of the air shall carry the voice, and that which hath wings shall tell the matter."

When evil is done, there are innumerable birds and other creatures with wings to tell what has been done!

One of the most powerful and moving scenes in all fiction is that in *Romola* where George Eliot describes the retribution that befell the pleasure-loving Greek, Tito Melema. He had wronged two women and publicly denied, and repudiated as a man he had never seen before, the foster-father who had brought him up and given him the jewels with which to purchase him out of slavery. Tito escaped from the angry mob in Florence by leaping into the Arno from the parapet of the bridge.

At length, exhausted and almost unconscious, he was flung up by the tide of the river amid the reeds on the bank, where the old foster-father, his mind reeling under the shock of the denial by his son, waited and hoped for vengeance. The old man had reason enough left to recognize Tito and strength enough left to clutch him by the throat with infinite satisfaction. At the close of that powerful scene, George Eliot writes: "Who shall lay his finger upon justice and say it is here? It is not without us as a fact. It is within us as a great yearning."

That certain sins find men out in time, even in the body, is a fact that must be apparent to everyone. The sins of appetite and the flesh leave an indelible mark upon the face, and even worse marks within the body. "He that soweth to his flesh shall of the flesh reap corruption" (Gal. 6:8). In the recollections of his college days at Amherst, former President Coolidge, speaking of some of his classmates, said:

"A small number became what we called sports. But they were not looked on with favor, and they have not survived. It seems to be true that unless men live right they die. Things are so ordered in this world, that those who violate its laws cannot escape the penalty. Nature is inexorable. If men do not follow the truth, they cannot live."

Whether in time a man's sin finds him out or not—that is, in exposure—it always finds him out in its effect upon his character. I do not refer now to the punishments of conscience; for whether the world finds out a man's sin or his conscience finds it out, *sin* always finds him out. Sin of any kind hurts and degrades the soul, and whatever may be said of particular acts or deeds that have been evil, character reveals itself. The most serious thing about sin is not what it does to a man, in the sense of his external relationships, but what it does *in* a man. That is the saddest thing about sin, what it does in a man, and how it profanes the temple of his life and character.

> Sin was never sinned in vain,
> The reddening scars remain
>   And make confession;
> Lost innocence returns no more;
> We are not what we were
>   Before transgression.

IN CONSCIENCE

Sin is sure to find men out in conscience. The world may not know or may not care, but conscience takes up its inexorable search and inflicts its unbribable judgments.

> Conscience, what art thou?
> Thou tremendous power,
> That dost inhabit us without our leave,
> And art within ourselves another self—
> A master-self, that loves to domineer
> And treat the monarch frankly as the slave.

"If it were done when 'tis done." But that is just the trouble with sin. It is never done. Where the world stops its inquiry or ends its judgments, and where nature may overlook, conscience is inexorable. Nothing is so remorseless as remorse. Sometimes the punishment of conscience is immediate. It was so in the case of Judas, who, as soon as he found that Christ was to be delivered up to death, came and flung the blood money down before the mocking priests. Their only remedy for the anguish of his soul was to say to him, "See thou to that." That is all this world, which tempts a man to sin, can ever do for the man who has yielded to the temptation. "What is that to us? What do we care about your troubled conscience? See thou to that."

The reaction of conscience was also immediate in the case of Peter. The moment he looked into the face of the amazed Savior, who had heard his cruel denial, he went out and wept bitterly. But sometimes conscience is chloroformed and dulled by the occupations or pleasures of the world, and sometimes by the very temporary delight which men get out of their transgressions. But this only means that the punishments of conscience will be all the more intense, and its exactions the more dreadful, when conscience finally awakes. Conscience may sleep in prosperity, only to awake in the storm of adversity.

Note what some perceptive people have said on the subject:

"He will easily be content and at peace whose conscience is pure."   *—Thomas à Kempis*

"Conscience tells us that we ought to do right, but it does not tell us what right is—that we are taught by God's Word."
                                              —Henry Clay Trumbull

"Labor to keep alive in your breast that little spark of celestial fire, called Conscience."   *—George Washington in* Moral Maxims

"A conscience void of offense before God and man is an inheritance for eternity."   *—Daniel Webster*

It is impossible for an evildoer to get safely by the judgment seat of conscience. Some of you may have seen grim Alcatraz Island, formerly a federal prison, in San Francisco Bay. One day a group of prisoners was being taken into the prison enclosure. They had all been searched at the receiving station. Then, one by one, and with a considerable distance between them, they were marched past the little guardhouse and through the gates into the prison. Several had passed; but as one prisoner was walking in, an order rang out, "Halt!" The guards took the man into the guardhouse, and after careful search drew out of his ear a minute saw. In the guardhouse was a powerful magnet, which, by its vibrations, disclosed the presence of any bit of metal on a prisoner who passed through the gates. So it is impossible for the evildoer to pass successfully by the deep scrutiny of conscience.

Conscience enslaves with fear, and makes "cowards of us all." "The wicked flee when no man pursueth" (Proverbs 28:1). The slightest coincidence may seem to the sinner to be evidence that another has knowledge of his guilty secret. "The sound of a shaken leaf shall chase them." What could be greater than the unhappiness of a man who has sinned and not only is punished for it in his own conscience but is in constant dread of exposure?

There is another fact about the punishments of conscience which is often overlooked. I have had men tell me frankly that they could take no part in the work and the activities of the church, in whose message and mission they so earnestly believed, because of the rebuke and scoffing of their own conscience. They are in the church only as so many silent tongues, interested, sympathetic, but inactive and silent spectators in this great battle between good and evil. Why so many deeply religious, penitent, and God-loving persons who take no part in the battle? Because when they attempt to do so, conscience with its thunderous whisper commands them to be silent. The sin of yesterday lays its paralyzing hand upon them and commands them to be still. Nothing could be sadder than these words that are never spoken, these noble deeds that are never done because of this specter of conscience.

In Thomas Hood's famous poem, "The Dream of Eugene Aram," the unhappy school usher is described as going out in the fields with his boys and, while they played at their games, sitting apart, reading a book which rested upon his knees.

> At last he shut the ponderous tome;
>   With a fast and fervent grasp
> He strained the dusky covers close,
>   And fixed the brazen hasp:
> "Oh God! could I so close my mind,
>   And clasp it with a clasp."

Alas, no human power can close or clasp that book which conscience so inexorably places before us and commands us to read.

In Eternity

Sin has a wide empire in which to reign and do its work. It has the visible field of time. It has the invisible and mysterious kingdom of conscience. But it also has the endless cycles of eternity. Sin finds men out in eternity. The moral laws which are at work in this life certainly do not cease to operate in the life to come. If man is a moral being, and if God conducts the affairs of the universe in righteousness and in justice, then there is certainly nothing strange about the fact that sin finds men out in eternity.

The Third Commandment has a great reason annexed to it, and that is, "For the Lord will not hold him guiltless that taketh his name in vain" (Exodus 20:7). This means: "However the breakers of this Commandment may escape punishment from men, yet the Lord our God will not suffer them to escape His righteous judgments." Suppose we grant, although it is contrary to the general law of experience, that a man's sin should not find him out in time, that no one should know his guilty secret, that it should leave no mark in his body. And suppose we grant that his seared conscience does not awaken to arraign him before its bar. Still he must reckon with the judgments of the life to come. Nothing could surpass in awe and solemnity the pronouncements of punishment upon sin in the world to come. The most solemn and awe-inspiring of those pronouncements come from the lips of Christ Himself. Men say that when He speaks about the worm that never dies and the fire that never goes out, He is using figures of speech. Of course He is. But what figures of speech they are! Metaphors which shake the soul! If the reality required that kind of a figure to express His meaning, then what must be that reality!

The plain statement, and the repeated statement, of Christ, the apostles, and the Scripture is that we will all stand before the Judgment Seat of God to give an account of our life here, every thought, every deed, and that the whole of the territory of our life will be uncovered and exposed in that judgment. As for the punishments, we know that we carry in our own breast all the necessary agents. In our conscience and in our memory we have all the necessary equipment for future punishment. Think of what memory can do!

What is this power
That recollects the distant past,
And makes this hour,
Unlike the last,
Pregnant with life,
Calling across the deep
To things that slumber, men that sleep?
They rise by number and with stealthy tread,
Like a battalion's tread,
Marshal our dead.

This is the gift
Men cannot bargain with nor shift,
Which went with Dives
Down to hell,
With Lazarus up to heaven,
Which will not let us e'er forget
The sin of years,
Though washed with tears;
Whate'er it be,
Men call it memory.

This is searching enough and solemn enough to make anyone think seriously of any kind of sin. The strong probability of its detection and exposure, the certainty of its disastrous effects upon character in this life, the certainty of the stings and pains which it will inflict through conscience, and the absolute certainty of its exposure and punishment in the life to come—all this is of a nature calculated to make people pray with a new and deep earnestness when they recite the Lord's Prayer, "Lead us not into temptation, but deliver us from the evil one." "My soul, be on thy guard!"

But I would not be giving the whole message of Christ or the gospel or the Scriptures, were I to stop here. I might warn many, but others I might leave plunged in melancholy and unhappy reminiscence. But, thank God, it is not necessary to stop here. Where sin has abounded, grace has much more abounded! If sin is the strongest, the darkest, the most terrible fact in life, it is matched by another fact, a fact mightier and stronger, and that is the fact of God's redeeming love, that the blood of Jesus Christ cleanseth us from all sin. God has not dealt lightly with sin, but He sent the great champion, His only Son, to meet it and to conquer it in the fearful battle of Calvary. Henceforth to those who repent and confess their sins and put their faith in Christ there is no more condemnation for sin. As far as the east is distant from the west, so far hath He put your sin from you. "Though your sins be as scarlet, they shall be as white as snow; though they be red like crimson, they shall be as wool" (Isa. 1:18).

2

CHOOSE YOU THIS DAY

Choose you this day whom you will serve (Joshua 24:15).

One hot August Sabbath in the north of Italy I stood by the parapet of an ancient bridge over a brown sluggish stream flowing towards the Adriatic. In the distance was the brown town of Rimini. Here and there in the river below me fishermen were drawing in their nets. It is not much of a river, and yet it is one of the most famous rivers in history. It was there, on another summer day, in 49 B.C., that Julius Caesar reined in his horses before he drove his chariot through the river.

The Roman senate, under the domination of Pompey, Caesar's rival, had ordered Caesar, who had won such splendid victories in Gaul, to disband his legions. That was the turning point in the career of Julius Caesar. The moment he received the tidings he started for the Rubicon, which was the dividing line between his province of Cisalpine Gaul and Italy proper.

Realizing the momentous decision he was about to make, Caesar paused for a little on the bank of the river. To himself and to his companions he said: "If I pass not this river immediately, it will be the beginning of all misfortune. The die is cast!" With that he drove his chariot into the river and stood on the Italian side, ready for battle and ready for destiny.

Men of feeble resolve never make their mark. Mental, moral, and spiritual invertebrates accomplish nothing because they can decide nothing. Asked how he conquered the world, Alexander

19

the Great answered: "By not wavering." The greatest conquest to which man is called—the conquest of eternal life in Christ—is also won by resolve and decision.

Joshua is one of the great hearts of the Old Testament and of the world. He was every inch the hero. Whether leading the spies into the Promised Land and making with Caleb the immortal minority report, or leading Israel across Jordan's flood, or in battle with Jericho and the bristling fortresses and hostile tribes of Canaan, or on his knees before the angel of the Lord, Joshua is the man who wins our admiration. He is loyal, obedient, courageous, faithful, and, above all, a man of decision and of immediate action.

The conquest of Canaan had been accomplished, and the land had been allotted to the several tribes. But now that the war was over, Joshua found that the people were declining toward idolatry, their ancient and hereditary sin. The local shrines of worship had corrupted the conquerors of the land. Realizing that his sun was low on the horizon, and that the days of his pilgrimage were almost over and that shortly he must engage in that last battle from which no man emerges the victor, Joshua called all the leaders of the nation together in a solemn general assembly at Shechem.

Although the tabernacle was at Shiloh, Shechem was the most sacred and most memorable place in Israel. It was there that Abraham, coming from the far East, had first settled, and there that God had renewed with him the Covenant. There Jacob had purchased his parcel of land; and there the bones of Joseph, which the dying patriarch had charged his people to carry with them out of Egypt, and which had accompanied the people in all their marches and battles in the wilderness, had been reverently deposited when the land was conquered. There Jacob had come when he returned from Padanaram, and there it was that the Lord had appeared unto him and told him to put away his idols and renew his vow at Bethel, where the Lord had met him thirty and more years before.

There it was, then, that Joshua convened the people. As he reviewed the history of the nation and pleaded with the people for loyalty to God, they could see on either side of the valley the two rugged peaks, Mount Ebal and Mount Gerizim, the mount of cursing and the mount of blessing. Obedient to the directions given him by Moses when the land had been taken, Joshua put six representatives of six tribes on Mount Ebal to pronounce the curses of the law, and six representatives of the six other tribes upon Mount Gerizim to pronounce its blessings.

What a stage was this for the general assembly of Israel and for Joshua's farewell! If you were to put Plymouth Rock and York-town and Lexington and Independence Hall together, you would not have what Shechem was to Israel.

Joshua went clear back to the fountain from which had flowed the stream of Israel's national life. He told the people how God had called Abraham out of Ur of the Chaldees, and the covenant he had made with him, the land he had given him. Then he traced the history of Isaac and of Jacob, the captivity in Egypt and the great deliverance, how God had put darkness between the people and the Egyptians at the Red Sea, and brought the sea upon them and covered them. Then the conquest of the tribes which lay on the other side of the Jordan, the crossing of the Jordan, the fall of Jericho, and victory after victory—but not, Joshua reminded them, "with *thy* sword, nor with *thy* bow." God had given them a land for which they had not labored, and cities which they built not to dwell in, and vineyards and oliveyards which they planted not.

The logical answer to this great history, the logical expression of the life of a nation, with which God had dealt as He had not dealt with any other people, was loyalty and obedience to God. Instead of that, the people were sinking into idolatry. Outwardly they were followers of the God of Israel, but many of them in their habits and in their worship were idolaters. Such a condition, Joshua told them, could not continue. They must decide whether they wanted to serve idols or to serve the living God.

Knowing that he could not choose or decide for them, Joshua told them to choose. He asked them to weigh the advantages of service to God or service to idols. If they thought it not good to serve Jehovah, then they could select the gods of their forefathers in the land where Abraham lived, or the gods of Egypt, or the gods of the Amorites whom they had conquered. But they must decide, and he called for an immediate decision. This day the nation must go solemnly on record for God or against Him. Regardless of their decision, Joshua told them his—even if he and his household were the only ones in the nation, still he would be faithful to God: "As for me and my house, we will serve the Lord."

When the people quickly expressed their preference for the God of Israel and their determination to serve Him, Joshua, knowing well the fickleness of the national heart, reminded them that it is not easy to serve God, that it involves obedience and sacrifice, and that if they really meant to choose God, then they must part with their idols. This the people agreed to do. The idols were brought forth from their hiding place and abandoned or destroyed. Rearing a great stone as a witness of their choice of God and their resolve to serve Him, Joshua said to the assembly: "Behold, this stone shall be a witness unto us; for it hath heard all the words of the Lord which he spake unto us: it shall therefore be a witness unto you, lest ye deny your God" (Joshua 24:27).

Edwin Markham has a poem in which he represents the Creator as looking upon man with all his gifts and powers and saying that these are not enough. To make sure that man can dare the vision and endure, God determines to test him by withdrawing His face, leaving only a broken clue, a crevice through which the glory glimmers, a footprint on the road, a whisper in the sky. God leaves man torn between the "No" and the "Yes":

> Drawn upward by the choice that makes him free—
> Leave him in tragic loneliness to choose,
> With all in life to win or all to lose.

WE MUST CHOOSE FOR OURSELVES

Joshua chose for himself, and chose in no uncertain terms: "As for me and my house, we will serve the Lord." But he knew that he could not choose for the tribes of Israel. They must choose for themselves. "Choose you this day whom ye will serve." Man is a social being. He is united to all humanity, and it is not good for man to be alone. Yet, in another sense, man, in his greatest moments, is alone.

> We are spirit clad in veils.
>   Heart by heart was never seen.
> All our deep communing fails
>   To remove the shadowy screen.

There is an inner sanctuary, a self within ourselves, where we retire from all other fellowship, comradeship, or influence. There is a lonely arena where by ourselves we pass through the great experiences of life. A man must face temptation alone, as Jesus faced it for Himself and for mankind in the desert. A man must bear the burden of his sin and guilt alone. Every man—how true it is—shall bear his own burden. A man must drink alone the cup of his sorrow. Like Christ he can say, "I have trodden the winepress alone." A man must face death alone as he goes down into the river where none may accompany him. And all alone a man must make the momentous decisions for time and for eternity. Others may persuade you, but cannot decide for you. Others may inspire you, but cannot control you. They can pray for you, but they cannot work out your destiny. You are the man! You have the choice! The vote is yours!

> Thou hast a choice; to choose is to create.
> Remember whose the sacred lips that tell,
> Angels approve thee when thy choice is well.

THE CHOICE INVOLVES SACRIFICE

The choice of eternal life and the decision for Christ is not without cost. Lest the people should be too impulsive and enthusiastic in their choice of Jehovah, Joshua reminded them what it meant. They must change their lives and abandon their idols. Eternal life is not to be compared in value with this world. No man can take both this world, in its lower meaning, and the world to come. It was uttered a long time ago, but the truth of it still stands: "No man can serve two masters." There are a great many professed followers of Christ who have given a sort of intellectual vote and decision for Christ, but who have not chosen Him with their hearts. Their hearts are still in the world and for the world.

A Christian must decide for himself. Nevertheless, it always saddens me when someone asks me, someone who is thinking about uniting with the church and confessing his faith in Christ, "Must I give up this? Must I give up that?" Generally they then mention some worldly custom or pleasure of society. Would God they would come the other way: "What *can* I give up for the sake of Christ who died for me?"

One of Bunyan's characters was Mr. Facing-Both-Ways. How many there are all about us like that! Another man of whom

Bunyan tells us was the boatman who faced in one direction and rowed in the other. A great many church members have their faces turned toward heaven, but they row in the other direction. If we are honestly and sincerely to choose God, we must be willing to believe that He is better than the world, and be ready to part with a few of the pleasures and spoils of the world for the sake of eternal life.

To Delay Makes the Right Decision More Difficult

To refuse today to do what conscience tells us we ought to do makes it more difficult for us to do it when conscience speaks to us again tomorrow. In proportion as men disobey conscience or the promptings of the Holy Spirit, their will becomes weak and impotent.

Indecision is itself a choice. Time decides for the man who will not decide for himself. If Caesar had remained searching his heart on the banks of the Rubicon, not knowing whether to obey the mandate of the senate or to cross and conquer, the armies of Pompey would have decided the matter for him, and decided it against him. A plane is to leave tomorrow for Europe at twelve o'clock, and you think you may go by that flight, and even have a reservation on it. But you are not quite sure whether you will take it or not, and turn the idea over in your mind today, tonight, and until one minute past twelve tomorrow. By that time the plane will have decided for you that you will not, and cannot, take that flight. Decisions are made, whether we make them or not. Time decides, if we will not. And time always decides against us. On the bypath of by-and-by, men arrive at the house of never.

The Time for Decision Is Limited

This life is a test and a trial, a probation for eternity. Youth is a probation for manhood. Today decides tomorrow. This hour decides what the next hour will be. Now is the time to decide, and no one knows how brief that period of "now" is. This day is your day. Neither you nor I know anything about tomorrow. We do know, however, that the time to choose for Christ and for eternity is limited. Christ Himself, in the most solemn words of which the divine lips were capable, expressed that truth when He told of those who came to the doors of the bridegroom's palace and found them shut: "And the door was shut."

When asked to renounce Christ or suffer death in the flames, the venerable Polycarp said: "For seventy and eight years I have served Him. He has never forsaken me. Now I will not forsake Him." Call the roll of all those who have chosen Christ, the roll of the living, the longer roll of the dead, and you will wait in vain to hear a single one who honestly and sincerely chose Christ rather than the world and followed Him, and who will testify that he made the wrong choice. The question for you to decide is: "Shall I make the right choice?"

Blind Bartimaeus, sitting by the walls of Jericho, which Joshua had conquered centuries before, heard that He who bore Joshua's name—Jesus—was passing by, and, despite the rebukes of the crowd, cried out, "Have mercy on me," and chose light rather than darkness. Saul of Tarsus heard His voice on the way to Damascus, and immediately obeyed the vision and chose Christ and eternal life. The penitent thief on the cross had just one chance, one offer of eternal life; but he used that chance and chose Christ and heard Jesus say, "Today shalt thou be with me in paradise" (Luke 23:43).

Whom will you choose? Which will you have? God or the world? "Choose you this day whom ye will serve."

Perhaps you have been living a self-centered and selfish life, cut off from the sorrows and also the joys of mankind. I call upon you to choose, to decide now whether you will continue on that lonely and unhappy path, or follow in the steps of Him who said, "It is more blessed to give than to receive" (Acts 20:35).

You are perhaps brooding over some real or fancied wrong that has been done you, and the thought of it rankles in your breast and depresses your Spirit. I call upon you to decide whether you will continue to let the sun go down on your wrath, or whether freely from the heart you will forgive, even as God for Christ's sake has forgiven you.

You are perhaps listening to the seductive voice of the tempter, and have not yet uttered the decisive and final "No." I call upon you to decide whether you will remain longer in that dangerous territory of hesitation and indecision, or say to the tempter now and finally, "Get thee behind me, Satan."

You are perhaps one about whom the chain of some evil habit has been slowly but inexorably winding itself. I call upon you to decide whether you will turn against that evil habit and conquer it with the help of God, or succumb to it and become its slave.

You have perhaps heard much about Christ but have never yet made the great decision for Christ. I call upon you to decide for Christ or against Him. Choose you this day between Christ and the world.

On the rugged, wave-beaten cliffs on the west coast of Scotland a man was once gathering the eggs of the sea birds which nested there. He had been let down from the top of the cliff by a rope to the ledge where the nests were, but in a moment of carelessness had let the rope slip from his hand. As it swung down and out and seaward, and then came swinging in again toward him, he knew that the first swing inward of the rope was his only chance, and that the next swing would be beyond his reach. With all the powers of body and mind and soul tense and alert, he stood on the edge of the ledge waiting for the rope to come in toward him. Just as it reached the end of its swing, he stretched out his hand, seized it, and was saved.

Every day, every hour, every moment, the swing of the rope of opportunity for choosing the good and great things of life—and the greatest and most important thing of all, repentance toward God and faith in Christ—becomes shorter and shorter. Do not wait for the next swing of the rope. "Seek ye the Lord while he may be found, call ye upon him while he is near" (Isa. 55:6). Choose now! Choose this day!

3

WHILE HE IS NEAR

Seek ye the Lord while he may be found, call ye upon him while he is near   (Isaiah 55:6).

One of the old Saxon kings set out with an army to put down a rebellion in a distant province of his kingdom. When the insurrection had been quelled and the army of the rebels defeated, the king placed a candle over the archway of his castle where he had his headquarters. Lighting the candle, he announced through a herald to all those who had been in rebellion against him that all who surrendered and took the oath of loyalty while the candle was burning would be spared. The king offered them his clemency and mercy, but the offer was limited to the life of that candle.

Every great offer of life and of time has its candle limitations. This is true of the offer of fortune and prosperity, or knowledge, or health, or affection. There is a limited period of time in which to make use of their offer and their opportunity. This is true most of all of the greatest offer ever made to man, the offer of eternal life through Jesus Christ, God's Son.

Isaiah 55 is one of the great invitation chapters of the Bible. It rings with that favorite word of God, "Ho, every one that thirsteth, come ye to the waters." This is a word which resounds in the Bible from the book of Genesis to the book of Revelation. When Noah had finished the ark, God said to him, "Come. . . into the ark." In the great parable of the supper Jesus represents God as saying to men, "Come, for all things are now ready." Christ Himself in unforgettable music said, "Come unto me, all ye that labor

27

and are heavy laden" (Matt. 11:28). This word "come" sounds through all the history and narrative and prophecy and warning and appeal and judgment and apocalypse of the Bible. It is the word that is written over the gates of heaven in letters of light to greet our pilgrim feet. And with this word, the divine revelation comes to a conclusion when John hears the voice of the angel using almost the very language of Isaiah, and saying, "The Spirit and the bride say, Come. . . . And let him that is athirst come. And whosoever will, let him take the water of life freely" (Rev. 22:17).

SEEK YE THE LORD

To seek the Lord is life's great, but greatly neglected, business. Men give their time and energy and strength and enthusiasm to other things and other quests, things which in the end fail and betray and disappoint the soul. The divine love here wonders at the way men seek something else rather than God. Inviting the soul to come to the waters and drink of the water of life, divine love says, "Wherefore, do ye spend money for that which is not bread and your labor for that which satisfieth not?" (Isa. 55:2).

But God never disappoints. The bread that He offers is real bread and the water that He offers is the water of life. Cardinal Wolsey in his dying hour exclaimed,

> Had I but served my God with half the zeal
> I served my king, He would not in mine age
> Have left me naked to mine enemies.

But where and when did you ever hear of a man who in the time of his defeat or overthrow or death regretted the time and search he had given to find God, or who said, "If I had only served myself as I have served my God, I would not now be left naked to my foes"? God made the soul, and the soul was made for God. And the soul will never be satisfied—with true and deep and abiding satisfaction—with anything but God. The great end of life is to know God and to be known of Him, and God can be found. The Bible rings with a thousand promises that if we seek God we shall find Him, and Christian history is bright with the illuminated letters of believers who testified that they tasted and found that God was good.

How to Seek the Lord

The way to seek God is charted in the Bible and in the history of believing souls. The roads that lead to God are clearly and unmistakably marked and "he that runs may read."

The Bible is one place where we seek God. It was given for that purpose. It is a lamp unto our feet and a light unto our path. How many men have found in the pages of the Bible the path that leads away from sin and brings the soul to God! The Bible speaks to the soul of man, for it was made for the soul, and the entrance of God's Word gives light. Jesus said, "Search the scriptures; for in them ye think ye have eternal life; and they are they which testify of me" (John 5:39). The Bible is a light which lights the way to God.

The Waldensian preachers sometimes traveled about as merchants and dealt in jewels and precious stones as a way of obtaining access to the families of the nobility. When they had disposed of their rings and trinkets and were asked if they had nothing more to sell, they answered, "Yes, we have jewels still more precious than any you have seen. We will be glad to show you these also if you will promise not to betray us to the clergy. We have here a precious stone so brilliant that by its light a man may see God. And another which radiates such a fire that it enkindles the love of God in the heart of its possessor." Then, unwrapping their bundle, they brought out a Bible. It is indeed the most precious of all precious stones, for by its light a man sees God and can find Him. That is the reason—and the only reason—for reading the Bible. That is why it is profitable and necessary every day to read the sacred page.

We can find God by *prayer*. God stands by His promise that they who seek Him in prayer will find Him. "Call upon me. . . I will deliver thee." Promise after promise flashes on page after page of the Bible that if we seek God we shall find Him, and that if we ask it shall be given unto us. Not that we get everything for which we ask, for that would often not be good for us, but that if we seek God in prayer we shall find His will for us and rejoice in it. How earnestly the prophets and the apostles, Abraham, Moses, Elijah, Samuel, Joshua, and David in his fall, sought God and found Him. How earnestly Christ sought God in prayer, in the desert place before it was day, on the mountaintop, in the Garden of Geth-semane, and in the last hour on the cross. If God is not real to you, how earnestly have you sought Him in prayer?

God is to be sought by *repentance*. To seek Him in the Bible, to seek Him in prayer, will not avail unless we seek Him also with repentance. "Seek ye the Lord while he may be found, call upon him while he is near." Then comes this word about repentance—"Let the wicked forsake his way, and the unrighteous man his thoughts: and let him return unto the Lord, and he will have mercy upon him; and to our God, for he will abundantly pardon" (Isa. 55:7).

There is no sincere seeking after God without repentance, for repentance is the evidence that the soul wants God more than the things of this world. For thirty years, perhaps, Jacob had failed to keep his vow to go to Bethel and worship, the vow that he had made when in his dream he saw the ladder reaching up to heaven and the angels of God ascending and descending upon it. Now, with his family sunk in idolatry, Jacob had settled down in the lush pastures of Shechem, more interested apparently in his flocks and herds than in seeking God or keeping the vow that he had made so many years before.

Then the voice of God spoke to Jacob, "Go up to Bethel, and dwell there" (Gen. 35:1). And Jacob arose and went to Bethel. But before he made that journey he destroyed and buried the idols which his family had accumulated. That was the proof that he was in earnest when he went to seek God at Bethel, and when he came to Bethel in repentance God appeared unto him again and blessed him. There is no doubt that one reason for the little knowledge of God that some people have and the little enjoyment of God which they experience is that they do not truly seek Him with repentance, that their religious profession and their Christian associations do not mean a change, an abandonment, a relinquishment, in their lives.

WHEN TO SEEK THE LORD

"Seek ye the Lord while he may be found." This gracious and tender invitation has an earnest and solemn note in it. God is to be sought after and found, not next week, nor next year, but today, while He is near, and while He may be found.

But is God not always near? Is He not closer than breathing? Is He not, as Paul said on Mars' Hill, "not far from every one of us"? In His providence and government God is always near to us. But there are times when God is near to us in grace, in our opportunity to reach out after God, to find Him and know Him as our Savior. There is a sense in which God cannot always be found, when He is not always near. Because this life is the time for seeking Him, and because our hearts change, there are times when we can and will seek after God, and there are times when we have no interest in Him.

IN SICKNESS

God is near to the soul in time of sickness. Sickness teaches us our weakness, our littleness, our dependence upon God. After he had preached for many years, Thomas Chalmers, the great Scottish preacher, had an illness that lifted him into a higher sphere and he soared aloft. God has private doors by which He enters men's lives, and one of those doors is sickness. How quickly the sky and the winds of life can change! Yesterday all was bright and fair and prosperous; today you are brought low. All your strength is spent and you learn how weak man is and how dependent upon God. In the time of sickness we make a new appraisal of life. How poor are some of the things that we have sought after, how rich the things we have neglected! Then we realize our shortcomings and our failures, the things we would like to change if we get well again, the things we will not do again that we have been doing, the things which we have left undone and which now we will do. God then is near. Call on Him!

IN SORROW

God is near in the time of sorrow. Sorrow is one of God's greatest ministers. Life without sorrow would be like earth without rain or dew. As in the beautiful figure of Isaiah, the rain comes down from heaven and the snow, and causes the earth to bring forth and bud, that it may give seed to the sower and bread to the eater, so is the rain of sorrow to the soil of life if we make use of it. What a preacher sorrow is! What chords it strikes! Then, for a time at least, the heart is softened, affections are purified, defiling passions spread their dark wings and depart, hatreds expire, and the soul moves Godward.

In my office as a minister it is my privilege to meet many souls in a time of sorrow, and I have often thought, if only now the soul would take this flood tide and sail on it! If only now, while it has the light, it would walk toward God, for now He can be found, now He is near! But so often the precious moment is lost, the rain of heaven is wasted, and the soul goes back to its old ways and its old life.

IN CONSCIENCE

God is near in conscience. Conscience is God's faithful oracle in the heart of man. As long as conscience can be troubled, there is the hope of spiritual health. And how and in how many ways, conscience often speaks to our souls. When, after the Fall, the man and the woman heard the voice of God walking in the garden, they were afraid, and hid themselves among the trees. What was it that made them afraid when God was near in the garden? It was conscience. When the prophet Nathan, with his matchless parable of the ewe lamb of the poor man slaughtered to feed the rich man's guest, awakened the conscience of David, the king knew that God was near and sought Him and His mercy in penitence and in prayer. When Herod heard of the preaching of Jesus and dismissed all other accounts and theories as to Jesus, and said, "It is John, whom I beheaded: he is risen from the dead" (Mark 6:16), it was conscience that was speaking within him.

There are men in the Bible who are like ships which emerge for a moment out of the mist into the sunlight and then again disappear into the mist and fog. I mean men like Herod, when he heard John preach; and Pilate, when Jesus stood before him; and Felix and King Agrippa, when Paul preached to them—men who had a special moment of divine grace, a truce of God, as it were, when their conscience was aroused, when they might have chosen Christ and eternal life, but turned away and disappeared into the darkness. They did not seek God while He could be found or call upon Him while He was near. I speak now as God's minister to that conscience, to that soul within you. You can hear, and you do hear, the voice of God. God offers you His grace, His pardon, His amazing love. What will you do with it? By so many ways, by so many providences—pain, sorrow, failure, joy, trouble, and tribulation—God draws nigh to your soul. "In an acceptable time have I heard thee" (Isa. 49:8).

WHEN GOD IS NOT NEAR

But God is not always near, in the first place, because the disposition of the person's heart and life changes. There is many a man, a stranger to Christ today, who can look back, if he is willing, to some hour or some experience in his life when he knew that God was near and that he was near to God, and he has never been that near again.

I once received into the church at a communion service a man over eighty years of age. He came to church for a time and then dropped out and went back to his old life. The explanation undoubtedly was this: He told me that when he was a youth in a boys' school in New England, the school was swept by a revival, and many of the boys were converted and took Christ for time and eternity. The voice of God spoke to him too and urged him to take Christ as his Savior, but he deliberately set himself against yielding and refused the call of God's Holy Spirit. God was near to him then, and never that near again. That was his hour. God said then, "Today! Now!" but he said, "Tomorrow!" And tomorrow never came.

This is the only life in which God draws nigh to us as our Savior, and the only life in which we can choose Him as our Savior. Men have asked the question: If a soul refuses the call of God in this life, and remains impenitent even unto death, is it not possible that in the life after death he should have another offer of salvation, and there, under new environment and new circumstances, and with a new vision of Christ, should repent and believe and be eternally saved? All that we can answer is that there is no indication or intimation of the second chance in the Scriptures. If that were so, then it would leave meaningless all the urgings and pleadings of Christ and the apostles and the Holy Spirit to choose God in this life. It would leave meaningless that large number of the parables of Jesus which deal with men in their relations to God and time and eternity, and leave man at death in his fixed and finished destiny.

Even if the gospel were preached to a man in the life to come, what possible forces or influences could work on him there and persuade him to choose God as his Savior, if in this life he heard the same gospel and refused to do so? What could be clearer, as an answer to that question, than those words of Jesus at the end of His great parable, when He said, "If they hear not Moses and the prophets, neither will they be persuaded, though one rose from the dead" (Luke 16:31).

Realizing that his own unhappy destiny was fixed and unchangeable, the rich man besought Abraham to send someone from the world of the dead to preach to his five brothers so that they might repent in time and escape the fate that had befallen him. Abraham reminded him that they had Moses and the prophets to listen to all their life, but he answered, "Nay, father Abraham, but if one went unto them from the dead, they will repent." It was as if he had said: "I had Moses and the prophets, but I paid no attention to them; but if someone had come from the dead and preached to me, I would have repented." But Abraham answered, and, of course, it is Christ who is speaking: "If they hear not Moses and the prophets, neither will they be persuaded, though one rose from the dead." In other words, there are no conceivable influences and forces working in the future life which could persuade a man to believe in Christ if he will not believe on Him in this life.

"Seek ye the Lord while he may be found, call upon him while he is near." The only life in which to seek God is this life, and in this life there are times of grace and special opportunity when God in His providence speaks to our soul, and we know and feel that He is near, and that we can and ought to choose Him. Those special opportunities, those special moments, those special hours, have their end, and time itself has its end, when, as Christ said, "And the door was shut." But now the door is open. Now the precious light of divine grace shines upon your path. While you have the light, walk in it. "Ho, everyone that thirsteth, come ye to the waters" (Isa. 55:1). "The Spirit and the bride say, Come. . . And let him that is athirst come. And whosoever will, let him take the water of life freely" (Rev. 22:17). "Seek ye the Lord while he may be found, call upon him while he is near."

4

ALONE

I have trodden the winepress alone   (Isaiah 63:3).

The shadows of the night are beginning to lift and flee away before the advent of the sun. Standing on the wall of some fortress in Israel and looking off in the direction of Edom, Israel's congenital and perpetual enemy, the watchman beholds a solitary warrior. The hastening day shows him to be grand in his stature, majestic in his movement, striding forward like a conqueror, with all his crimson garments streaming in the wind. As he draws nearer, the astonished watchman calls to him:

"Who is this that cometh from Edom, with dyed garments from Bozrah, this that is glorious in his apparel, travelling in the greatness of his strength?" (Isa. 63:1a).

"I that speak in righteousness, mighty to save" (Isa. 63:1b), comes the answer.

"Wherefore art thou red in thine apparel, and thy garments like him that treadeth in the winefat?" (Isa. 63:2).

"I have trodden the winepress alone; and of the people there was none with me."

Christian belief has always seen in this sublime Isaian passage a description of the triumph of Christ in His redeeming work, and the thing which has always impressed most the eye of him who looks upon this great portrait is not the majestic mien of the conqueror, nor his garments crimson from the battle, but his solitude, his utter loneliness: "I have trodden the winepress alone;

and of the people there was none with me; . . . and I looked and there was none to help" (Isa. 63:3, 5).

Loneliness is an inevitable portion of our human lot. Each life is an adventure by itself. No two people ever repeat the same experience. There is a constitutional loneliness which belongs to all men, for "the heart knoweth his own bitterness; and a stranger doth not intermeddle with his joy."

> Not even the tenderest heart, and next our own,
> Knows half the reason why we sigh or smile;
> Each in his hidden sphere of joy or woe,
> Our hermit spirits dwell and reign apart.
>
> *—John Keble*

There is a loneliness of place and a loneliness of state. Robinson Crusoe, cast on his lonely isle, has drawn after him the compassion of succeeding generations. But there is a loneliness of state that is quite different from the loneliness of place. Many a man has had his loneliest moments, not in solitude, but when walking the streets of some strange city, where there is a flash and glitter of fashion, and where one hears the roar of traffic, and a multitude of feet beat on the sidewalk like falling rain. There is much in that old saying, "Never less alone than when most alone, never more alone than when least alone." Thus man's loneliness is a link of human fellowship. But let us think, not of man's loneliness, but of the loneliness of Christ—first in the greatness and purity of His character, second in His temptations, and third in His sufferings for sin. Let us look now at this grand and solitary Sufferer.

THE LONELINESS OF CHRIST'S GREATNESS

Some years ago I climbed the highest mountain in southern California. When we reached the summit we found nothing but a heap of rocks and trampled sand. Not a tree, not a blade of grass, not a stump or shrub, not a living creature. There absolute silence reigned—a solemn awe-producing silence, which seemed to carry one clear back to the dawn of creation. On the mountain peak there was absolute solitude. The people and the noises of the world were far below us, where we could neither see them nor hear them.

So it is in life. The higher you climb, the lonelier it becomes. Elevation of soul separates from the crowd. The very elevation of a man's character, no matter how social and humanitarian he himself may be, and how noble his efforts for mankind, that very elevation of soul may repel men as well as attract them. The conviction men have that here is an incorruptible soul, one who will not compromise with iniquity, serves to separate that man from them. The grandest men of history have been the loneliest. Men like Moses, on the mount alone with God; Elijah, standing alone for God in a wicked and corrupt generation; Jeremiah, appointed to stand as an iron pillar and a brazen wall against a whole nation; John the Baptist, letting the thought of God take hold of him in the desert; Paul, after his glorious life for mankind, deserted and forsaken in the prison at Rome.

> Count me o'er earth's chosen heroes—they were souls that
>   stood alone,
> While the men they agonized for hurled the contumelious stone.

Because of the grandeur and purity of His soul Christ trod the winepress alone. He was altogether alone in His knowledge of the great redemptive work that He had come to do. Sometimes in a family where the stroke of death has fallen and the head of the family and the breadwinner has been laid low, you have seen little children, either playing about with indifference or looking curiously up into the faces of their elders, trying vainly to understand their sorrow and distress. Perhaps in a packet of old letters you have come across a paragraph which let you know that your father and mother had hours of deep concern and care concerning the welfare of the home and the education of the children, which you at the time never considered, and if you had thought of it, could not have understood. As to the great purpose and work of Christ when He was on earth, those about Him were no more than little non-understanding children. To His father and mother He said at the very beginning, when they rebuked Him for remaining behind in Jerusalem, "Wist ye not that I must be about my Father's business?" (Luke 2:49). His own mother, His own brethren did not understand Him and even when, in the most careful and deliberately chosen language, He spoke to His disciples about His redeeming work and what it would cost Him, they did not understand the saying.

Yes, it was a lonely way that Christ trod, from the time of His baptism and temptation to the hour of His final cry on the cross.

THE LONELINESS OF CHRIST'S TEMPTATIONS

Temptation is another link of human fellowship, for all are tempted. From that arena of combat none is exempt, and from that warfare there is no discharge, either honorable or dishonorable. Temptation is a lonely experience. Although the temptations are in a sense the same, and the sins that follow the temptations the same as they have been through all the generations, every man's temptation is for him an absolutely new and solitary experience. The tempter takes a man apart from all others. The scene of temptation, whether it be a crowded street, a busy office, a quiet study, or a country lane where the branches meet overhead, is always a wilderness, a desert place, where man meets the tempter alone, and where, in a moment of time, he can suffer irreparable loss or win incalculable profit and strength.

But let us look now at the temptation of Jesus. In that temptation there is a mystery which is the mystery of His divine person. The inspired author of the letter to the Hebrews says that He "was in all points tempted like as we are, yet without sin" (4:15). No doubt you have often pondered over that verse. It is true that Christ took upon Himself the form of a servant, and was made in all things like unto His brethren, and as such He was subjected to temptation. But to what degree His temptations were like ours, and whether, when the inspired penman said that He was tempted in all points like as we are, he meant "like" merely in the sense of the fact and the principle of temptation, or "like" us also in the detail of temptation—that is, whether Christ in His human nature was tempted as man is tempted to anger, to impatience, to hatred, to avarice, to cowardice, to evasion of duty, to falsehood, and to impurity—as to that, who can say? That is a subject into which we cannot, we must not, we dare not enter.

What we do know about the temptation of Jesus is that He was tempted as to the great purpose and work that He had come to do. And in that temptation He was terribly alone. The desert place, the wilderness of which the evangelists speak when they tell of His temptation by the devil, is more than just a geographical loneliness. It describes also the moral loneliness of Christ. "The spirit driveth him into the wilderness." There He was altogether alone in His encounter with Satan, when the destinies of redemption hung in the balance. As the evangelist graphically puts it, "he was with the wild beasts" (Mark 1:13).

Successful in the first and critical encounter with Satan, having bound the strong man, Christ went forth to spoil the goods of his house and to do His work of emancipation for the human soul. But have you ever paused over that verse with which Luke concludes his account of the Temptation—"And when the devil had ended all the temptation, he departed from him for a season" (4:13)? That leaves one with the impression that the tempter did not give up the battle after that first repulse. We wonder when and how the Prince of Darkness assailed Jesus again during His ministry. What we know is that whatever attempts he made were frustrated as they had been at the beginning, for Christ said, "The Prince of this world cometh, and hath nothing in me" (John 14:30). We know that the final assault of Satan was made at the very end of our Lord's life on earth, that hour of which Christ said, "This is your hour, and the power of darkness." As Satan had tempted Him in the beginning by the allurements of the world, so at the end Satan made one last effort to tempt Him in His sufferings.

The first act in that final temptation took place in the Garden of Gethsemane. In utter solitude, although He craved the companionship of His disciples, and besought them to watch with Him, Jesus entered into His agony, and sweat, as it were, great drops of blood, praying, "If it be possible, let this cup pass from me" (Mark 14:36). But whatever the temptation to turn aside from the great act of redemption on the cross, toward which He had hitherto steadfastly set His face, Jesus repulsed the tempter, and, as angels came and ministered to Him after His first victory over the tempter in the wilderness, so now we read, "There appeared an angel unto him from heaven, strengthening him" (Luke 22:43). When we listen to that mysterious cry that broke the stillness and pierced the darkness of Calvary, "My God, My God, why hast thou forsaken me?" (Matt. 27:46), we wonder if this was the final assault of Satan. If it was, we are not left in doubt as to the victory of Christ, for after that cry, "Why hast thou forsaken me?" came that beautiful and final and trusting prayer, "Father, into thy hands I commend my spirit."

Christ met and conquered the tempter alone that you and I might never need to meet him alone. In every battle with temptation He is our helper and our friend, because, having been tempted and having Himself overcome, He is now able to come to the aid of them who are tempted.

THE LONELINESS OF CHRIST'S SUFFERINGS

The agony of Christ in the Garden of Gethsemane and His agony on the cross outdistance all human suffering and woe. But here again suffering is another link in human fellowship, for all suffering is solitary and not to be shared by another. Others can sympathize, encourage, and be amazed, but every man drinks that cup by himself. Christ was lonely too in that by reason of the purity of His soul He alone had an understanding of what sin is and the ruin it had wrought in man's nature. Heaven hides from all eyes but its own that awful sight, a naked human heart. The nearer to perfection a soul is, the more sensitive it is to sin. The anguish of a Christian soul who has been betrayed by Satan into sin is far keener and greater than that of one who sins continuously and without distress or compunction of conscience. Who can tell, then, what the distress of Christ must have been as He moved amid his fallen creation? Once or twice we have an intimation of it as when He wept over the grave of Lazarus, and again when, about to heal the deaf and dumb boy, He looked up to heaven and sighed.

The sufferings of Christ were foreseen and anticipated sufferings. In that respect He differed from all others. Man must drink his cup of trial and suffering before his mortal probation is ended; but it is a merciful provision that he does not foresee and anticipate those sufferings. They are difficult enough when they come; but how much harder they would be if we were compelled to behold them and anticipate them before they came.

Suppose we had the power to lift the veil that screens the future. It is a good thing that we do not have that power. It is a good thing for all of us that we cannot foresee the future. But the sufferings of Christ were anticipated and foreseen. His face was always set toward the cross. He had a baptism with which to be baptized, and how His soul was straitened until it was fulfilled! Frequently He told His disciples that He must suffer many things of the scribes and Pharisees and be put to death. When at length the hour struck, He prayed, "The hour is come. . . . Father, save me from this hour" (John 12:27). And as in the Garden of Gethsemane He contemplated the dread ordeal which awaited Him on the cross, He said, "My soul is exceeding sorrowful, even unto death" (Matt. 26:38).

All the humiliation and suffering of Christ came to its terrific climax of loneliness on the cross, where He became "obedient unto death" and "bare our sins in his own body on the tree" (1 Peter 2:24). There He poured out His soul unto death. Now He met the actual and final fact to which He so often referred and toward which in His life upon earth He was ever marching. All that He bore in drinking our cup and in bearing the penal sufferings upon sin, you and I can never know. The only measure we have by which to measure them is the cry that broke the stillness on the cross, "My God, my God, why hast thou forsaken me?" But now the long battle is over. Now the great work is done. "It is finished!" He cries in triumph to heaven and earth and hell. All alone, unto the end, He has trodden the winepress of the wrath of God upon sin. And now from that winepress flows the red wine for a world's renewal and cleansing and redemption.

CONCLUSION

What we have been speaking of—the loneliness of Christ as our Redeemer—is not just a fact by itself in the religious history of our Lord. It is the great and practical fact for you and me. Christ was made the perfect Redeemer through His sufferings, and now for the sufferings of death He is crowned with honor and glory. The loneliness of Christ as our Redeemer proclaims the worth of man, the eternal majesty of a human soul. If this was undergone by Christ for the sake of man, then of what inestimable value is a man's soul? We judge the worth of the soul and the dignity and value of human nature not merely by the test of the purpose and design of life, not merely by the test of subtraction, that is, what man would be without a soul, and not merely by the test of endurance, that is, that the soul of man outlives the sun, the moon, and all the stars, but most of all by the price that the Lord Jesus Christ, the Son of God, paid for the redemption of the soul.

In the second place, the lonely sufferings of Christ as our Redeemer are the measure of our sin and of our need. If anyone is tempted to be careless and indifferent about the present state or future welfare of his soul, let him remember that it was the state of man's soul, and the future judgment which awaits it, that filled the Son of God's soul with anguish and grief inexpressible. He knows what the soul is worth, and He knows what it means for a soul to be excluded from the face of God.

Finally, the lonely sufferings of Christ are the ground of our hope. He returns in triumph from His great conquest on the cross, traveling in the greatness of His strength, mighty to deliver and mighty to save. Because He trod the winepress for us alone, we are never left alone. There are things that man must do alone. He must fight the battle of temptation alone. He must kneel in His Gethsemane and drink the cup of sorrow alone. He must meet God in judgment alone. No other can be with us or help us in these dread hours. Yet we have the help and the presence of Christ, who trod His winepress alone and walks by our side when we tread ours.

> The soul that on Jesus hath leaned for repose,
> I will not, I will not, desert to his foes.

5

IT IS FINISHED

It is finished (John 19:30).
It is done (Revelation 21:6).

Both phrases, "It is finished" and "It is done," were spoken by Christ, and both were heard by John: the first when he stood near the cross and in the darkness of the ninth hour heard Jesus cry out with a great voice, "It is finished"; the second when, in the vision granted unto him on the Isle of Patmos, he stood before the throne at the end of the ages and heard the triumphant Christ say, "It is done." The first cry, "It is finished," proclaimed that the foundation of the temple of redeemed humanity had been laid; the second cry, "It is done," proclaimed that the glorious structure had been completed. Between the two cries stretches the history of the church.

"It is finished." That is the greatest proclamation ever made to man. Yet it did not seem so when it was spoken. Just a derided, mocked, forsaken, broken, thorn-crowned, wounded, bleeding, dying Man. Who cares what He has finished? And who cares what His last cry is? Yet the world has never forgotten it. That cry, "It is finished," was heard by heaven, earth, and hell. Today it echoes around the walls of our churches, and at the end of the ages we shall hear it uttered, not from the cross, but from the throne, "It is done."

What had been finished? What is the meaning of that strange cry out of the silence and darkness that gathered about the cross on which Christ died? It means, first of all, that the sufferings of Christ are ended. A very real part of those sufferings, although not

43

the greatest part, was His physical suffering, for God gave Him a body, and in that body He suffered.

The Sufferings of Christ

Deep, deep is the mystery and sacrament of suffering. Everywhere in life and in the world it meets us and perplexes us and confuses us. Yet I am sure that in the end it will be seen that suffering has done great and beautiful things for mankind. We know that it is by suffering that the greatest things have been done by man for man; and the cross tells us that it is by suffering that the greatest thing has been done by God for man.

The cross was a method of punishment and death invented by a cruel people, the purpose of which was not only to inflict death, but to inflict it with the greatest possible degree of suffering. In this respect the cross did not fail of its purpose. All that the twenty-second psalm, from which Christ quoted on the cross, has to say about the sufferings of crucifixion—the terrible thirst, the bones out of joint, the heart like wax, the strength dried up like a potsherd, the tongue cleaving to the jaws, the protruding bones—all was fulfilled in the crucifixion of Christ. But now all that is over. His sufferings are ended. The Son of God will never suffer again.

The sufferings of Christ in the sense of His humiliation are ended. In the Incarnation, and in His great quest after the souls of men, Christ humbled Himself and was made in the fashion of a man, and became obedient to death, "even," says the apostle, "the death of the cross," that shameful, disgraceful, painful, and infamous death, "*even* the death of the cross." What it meant for Christ to assume our fallen nature, and to dwell constantly with sinners, only Christ could know.

> Heaven's Sovereign saves all beings but Himself
> That hideous sight—a naked human heart.

Not only did Christ dwell with sin, but, mystery of mysteries, He was made sin on our behalf. This alone can explain that agony in the Garden of Gethsemane. If Christ was shrinking merely from the physical pain of the Crucifixion, if that was what He meant by His cup, when He prayed, "Let this cup pass from me," then many a martyr, many a soldier on the field of battle has met death with greater fortitude and courage than Jesus. But what He was shrinking from was that identification with the sinner that was necessary before He could make atonement for him. But now that humiliation is over. It is finished. Christ will be raised up in glory. He will ascend into the heavens and sit at the right hand of God.

The sufferings of Christ in the sense of His loneliness are ended. Christ was the most loving, the friendliest person who ever lived. And yet, strange to say, as sometimes happens to the most loving—although for a different reason with Christ—He was the loneliest man who ever trod the earth. In spite of His careful predictions and explanations about the purpose of His coming, and the great work He was to do on the cross, the disciples "understood not" what He said. There was none with whom He could have fellowship and communion as to the great purpose of His death; not even with John, who leaned on His breast at the supper.

I suppose that was the reason why God broke the seals of the world of the departed souls and called up Moses and Elijah to stand on the mount and talk with Christ about His decease that He was to accomplish at Jerusalem. His enemies hated Him without a cause, and in spite of His love and fidelity to them, His friends and disciples forsook Him and fled. Truly Christ could say through the prophet Isaiah, "I have trodden the winepress alone."

But now the loneliness of Christ is over. "It is finished." Now He will have the company of His Father in heaven, of the angels and the archangels, and the souls of redeemed men made perfect in righteousness through the blood of His atonement. Ended too is His humiliation. Finished too are all His sufferings. Come, Joseph of Arimathea and Nicodemus, late in your devotion, and take His body down from the cross and lay it away, wrapped in the linen cloth, in that rock-hewn tomb where never yet man lay. Come, women who loved Him and followed Him, come with your spices and anoint His body for burial. Come, Mary, His mother, with the sword piercing your heart, for your Son's cruel sufferings are over. Come, Mary of Magdala, and take up your vigil at His grave. "It is finished!"

The Atonement of Christ Was Finished

All those sufferings, as we have seen, were ended when Christ cried on the cross at the ninth hour, "It is finished." But what was the meaning of those sufferings? The fact that one suffered greatly is not sufficient to explain why His last cry, "It is finished," still resounds in the world today, and will echo about the throne of God in the last great day.

Why did Christ suffer? Why did it behoove Him to suffer all these things? It was the great work of atonement that Christ had finished. He alone, of all men, came into the world to die, and His death on the cross was the price of man's redemption and forgiveness. It was a work that was begun from before the foundations of the world, for Christ is the Lamb of God that taketh away the sins of the world. But that great work reached its climax and consummation on the cross.

The promise that God gave to man when he fell; the covenants that He made with Noah and Abraham; the calling of a man, of a family, then a nation; the deliverance out of Egypt; the giving of the Law and the Ten Commandments; the tabernacles and the temple with their altars and their sacrifices; the miracles and judgments and symbols; the far-off flashings of the lights of prophecy; the preaching of John the Baptist; the song of the angels when Christ was born; His presentation in the temple, the silent years at Nazareth; His baptism in the Jordan and by the Holy Spirit; His temptation in the wilderness; His parables and miracles; His prayers, His tears, His sighs, His Last Supper; His betrayal by Judas, His denial by Peter, His condemnation by Pilate—all this, up to the last nail that was driven into his body, and the spear that was driven into His side—all this was a part of the great work of redemption, of reconciliation, for "God was in Christ, reconciling the world unto himself" (2 Cor. 5:19). Now all that work is finished. And Christ, seeing that all things were accomplished, cried out with a great voice, "It is finished."

Today the emphasis seems to have been shifted from what Christ did for man on the cross to what man can do for himself. Wherever this has taken place, there has gone with it a decline in vital faith, in personal conviction, and in enthusiasm for the Kingdom of God; for the cross is the one great fountain of true morality, of Christian joy, and of Christian enthusiasm. Ideals are very good, but in the straits of the soul, when we come into deep waters, we want something more than that. Only the finished work of Christ will do in that hour. In the cross there is strength for every hour and defense against every peril. Amid the world's gathering gloom and darkness the only hope is the cross of Christ and the work of redemption that was completed there when Christ cried, "It is finished."

THE KINGDOM OF SATAN WAS FINISHED

The war against evil was ended. There are many today who take pessimistic views as to the future of mankind. And no wonder, for they base their reliance on the theory of inevitable and invincible progress. Now they began to see that there is no such thing. If that is all we have to count upon, then all we can expect is the perpetual recurrence of what now is, or, worse than that, retrogression, decline, and decay. Some, therefore, are concluding that there is no great goal for mankind, no golden age, and that the beast is to be the perpetual companion of man.

But Christian faith casts a different horoscope. The treasures of inspiration are exhausted by the inspired penmen of the Scriptures as they describe the beauty and the glory of the day which is to come, a day so bright and glorious and splendid that, compared with it, the brightest day which has yet dawned upon the world is as midnight, and the fairest splendors which have invested the earth but as the shadow of darkness. This great Christian hope is based upon the triumph of Christ on the cross when He cried, "It is finished." The war against Satan, against the kingdom of evil, was finished. The seed of the woman, in the person of Christ, there bruised the head of the serpent.

But, men will ask, how can this be? We see no diminution of the power of the forces of darkness. We see Jerusalem everywhere battling with Babylon. We see everywhere the curse and the ravages and the new disguises and deceptions and deceits of Antichrist. Upon what ground, they ask, do you base this hope of a regenerated humanity? We base it upon the finished work of Christ upon the cross. When Christ died with that final cry on His lips, it did, indeed, look like an overthrow rather than a conquest, a defeat rather than a victory. Yet it was a great victory, but a new kind of victory, a victory won by death.

When the Philistines had blind Samson led out of his dungeon and into their palace and temple to make sport for them, so they might mock at him and at the God of Israel, Samson asked the lad who led him by the hand to let him feel the pillars upon which the temple stood, so that he might rest himself. Then he put one arm around one pillar and one arm around the other; and with a prayer to God, "O Lord God, remember me, I pray Thee, and strengthen me, I pray Thee, only this once" (Judges 16:28), Samson bowed himself with all his might; and the house fell upon his Philistine captors and tormentors. So it was on Calvary. With eyes blinded with love for mankind, Christ put one arm around the dark pillar of sin, and the other arm around the dark pillar of death, and then bowed Himself with all His might, even unto death, and Satan's empire fell.

But, says one, I see no signs of that fall. But wait! Remember that other cry, "It is done." John, who heard Christ cry on the cross, "It is finished," now stands at the end of the ages. The long conflict between good and evil has come to an end. Every engine of war and commotion has fallen, and the discord and strife of sin have been succeeded by infinite and universal peace. That trinity of deceivers, the beast, the false prophet, and the dragon, have been cast into the lake of fire. The new heaven and the new earth have taken the place of the old, and the new Jerusalem, the city of God, has come out of heaven like a bride adorned for her husband. Then John heard one who sat upon the throne say, "It is done." It was Alpha and Omega, the same who died upon the cross, and who, as He died, cried out, "It is finished." Now all that for which He died has been accomplished, and the cry of Christ on Calvary is answered by the cry of Christ upon the throne of the universe, when the kingdoms of this world have become the kingdoms of our Lord and of His Christ, "It is done."

And mystery of mysteries! O divine condescension! O unfathomable love! This great work which took in all the plan of God through the ages, all the sufferings of Christ on the cross, was done for *you*. It was done for *me*. The greatest hour of the soul comes when it answers that cry, "It is finished," and that cry, "It is done," by its own word of faith and belief and love, says, "It is done! It is done! 'The great transaction's done! I am my Lord's, and He is mine!'"

6

I AM NOT ASHAMED

For I am not ashamed of the gospel of Christ: for it is the power of God unto salvation to every one that believeth (Romans 1:16).

Deep in the heart of the Virginia mountains stands an ancient stone church. In the quiet acre along the side, close to the wall of the church, sleep the pioneer forefathers who conquered the wilderness with rifle, ax, and psalmbook. It is as if they are craving in death the fellowship of God's house which they enjoyed in life. In the stone over the portals of the church are cut these words: "This church was built by God-fearing inhabitants of this place as a token of their love for the Holy Gospel of our Lord Jesus Christ." What is said there concerning the building of that mountain church is true of all churches through all the ages. They were built by men "as a token of their love for the Holy Gospel of our Lord Jesus Christ."

Paul had preached the gospel in Tarsus, where he was born; in Jerusalem, the world's holy city; in Damascus, the world's oldest city; in Antioch, the golden city on the Orontes; in Ephesus, where the world's greatest temple, the Temple of Diana, stood; in Athens, the city of the mind and the home of the philosophers; and when he wrote this letter to the Romans he was preaching the gospel in Corinth, the metropolis of Greece. But not yet had he preached the gospel at Rome, the heart of the world. It had long been his desire and ambition to go to Rome and preach the gospel of Christ there. "I must see Rome," had been the determination of his mind; but every time he planned to go to Rome something came up to prevent him. Unable to go to the city in person, he writes this letter to the church and the Christians at Rome.

Because of his frequent failures to get to Rome, there were some apparently who were taking the view that Paul was reluctant or afraid to come to Rome and preach there. It was as if they had said, "Paul can preach the gospel at Jerusalem and Antioch and Athens and Corinth, but he will find it is a different matter to preach the gospel at Rome, the mighty capital of the world, with its grandeur, its cruelty, its wickedness, its superstition, its pomp, and its power."

If this was in their minds, Paul corrects that misunderstanding by his bold affirmation: "I am ready to preach the gospel to you that are at Rome also, for I am not ashamed of the gospel of Christ: for it is the power of God unto salvation." He told them in effect: "You talk to me about the power of Rome; and well do I know that power, for I am a citizen of Rome and proud of it. I have walked over Rome's great highways and chasm-spanning bridges, and everywhere I have seen the dust of its marching legions, carrying out the commands of the emperor. I know the power of Rome, but I do not fear it, for I know of a power that is greater than the power of Rome, and that is the power of the gospel of Christ, the power of God unto salvation."

These great words of Paul, how he was not ashamed of the gospel of Christ, and why he was not ashamed of it—because it was the power of God unto salvation—are a tonic for us today. We need a new and soul-refreshing conviction of the power of the gospel of Christ, a new and soul-refreshing pride in its beauty, its majesty, and its glory. It is the same gospel which Paul believed and preached, and you and I today have the same reasons that he had for not being ashamed of it. Indeed, because of the triumphs of the gospel since that age when it was preached by Paul, we have even greater reasons than Paul had for not being ashamed of it.

Not Ashamed of Christ

I am not ashamed of the gospel because I am not ashamed of Him whom it proclaims, its divine founder, our Lord and Savior Jesus Christ.

I am not ashamed of the fact that Christ is the eternal Son of God, and that He who thought it not robbery to be equal with God, emptied Himself and humbled Himself and was made in the likeness of sinful man for the salvation of the world. There are those who tell us that the main thing is to endeavor to do the will of Christ, and that one's rank will take care of itself. But that will not do for me. I must have a Christ who cannot only teach me and guide me and inspire me, but a Christ who can save me, and only the Son of God can do that. If I need a Savior, then why should I be ashamed of the fact that that Savior is very God of very God, the everlasting Son of the Father?

I am not ashamed of the great miracle by which Christ came into the world, that the eternal Son of God became man by taking to Himself a true body and a reasonable soul, being conceived by the power of the Holy Ghost in the womb of the Virgin Mary and born of her, yet without sin. I am not ashamed of that great constituent miracle which qualified Him to become the world's Redeemer.

I am not ashamed of the miracles of Christ. If you get rid of His miracles you get rid of Christ, for the only Christ we know is the One who worked great miracles. The evidence that He walked on the sea is just the same that He walked on the land, and the evidence that He raised the dead is just the same as the evidence that He Himself died on the cross and rose again from the dead. No, I am not ashamed of His miracles, not ashamed of the fact that they certify to His divine power and prove, as He Himself said, "that the Son of Man hath power on earth to forgive sins." I am not ashamed of the mercy and compassion and pity of God which the miracles reveal; that they opened the eyes of the blind to the beauty of earth and sky; that they opened the ears of the deaf to the music of the wind and the rain and the human voice; that they comforted and healed the brokenhearted. I am not ashamed of the prophecy and the prediction of the miracles of that day when man shall have put on immortality, and shall be restored to the lost image of God.

I am not ashamed of the precepts and teachings of Jesus. The words of other speakers and writers are like words cut on stones and monuments, but the words of Jesus are like the wind which blows wherever it desires. The systems and schemes and philosophies of men have blossomed and withered and disappeared like the leaves of the forests, but the words of Jesus are ever green. He never wrote a line save in the dust. Yet the words that He spoke have brought more hope and joy and righteousness into the world than all the sayings of all the wise men of all ages. Jesus said: "Heaven and earth shall pass away, but my words shall not pass away" (Matt. 25:35). The nearly two thousand years which have passed since He said that have only served to confirm the truth of what Jesus said. Find me a saying of Jesus that is obsolete. Find me a word of Christ that needs revision, that is no longer applicable to the needs and desires, the sins and passions, the sorrows and griefs of mankind. And then—but not until then—will I be ashamed of the teachings of Christ.

I am not ashamed of the example of Jesus, the new way of life which He taught men to take. Age cannot wither and custom cannot stale His infinite variety. In the womb of the morning He has the dew of His strength. I am not ashamed of the fact that after the world has come out of the most terrible war of history, a war which turned the sun into darkness and the moon into blood, it has become increasingly clear that the hope for men and nations is not in education, in science, in systems of government, in treaties, and in conferences, but in the way of righteousness and justice and peace and good will which the Man of Galilee taught. All other ways have been tried and failed. Today, amid the world's darkness, with the same love that made Him die on the cross, stands the Son of Man saying to mankind, "This is the way, walk ye in it." Will men take His way, or will they again try the golden portals of the future with the blood-rusted key of the past?

I am not ashamed of Christ as a friend. What a wonderful friend He is! I am ashamed of the fact that so often I have been unworthy of His friendship and faithless to Him. But of Him I am not ashamed. How could I be ashamed of a friend so loving, so patient, so understanding, so tender, so kind, a friend who speaks to the better nature in me, a friend who comes to seek me when I have gone astray, a friend who "sticketh closer than a brother" (Prov. 18:24)?

No, I am not ashamed of Christ. I am not ashamed of His complete deity, His miracles, His precepts, His beautiful and fadeless example, the way of life that He taught. I am not ashamed of

Him as a friend. Not until midnight shall blush to own a star. Not until tree or flower is ashamed of the sun of springtime that calls it forth into life and beauty, shall I be ashamed of Him who speaks to my soul and bids me live anew. Write as high as you will the names of the greatest actors on the stage of human affairs, and over them the name of the wisest of the sons of men, and over them the names of the saintliest and purest of mankind. Let these names shine with all the glory and beauty which are due them, and over them all, across the sky of the world which He created and redeemed, I will write, with a pen dipped in His blood, the name which is above every name, the blessed name of Christ.

Not Ashamed of the Gospel of Christ

Paul did not say, "I am not ashamed of Christ," but, "I am not ashamed of the gospel of Christ." And that means a great deal more. There are many who will praise Christ as a teacher, as a beautiful character, perhaps even as divine, but who are ashamed of His gospel. And what is that gospel? It is the message of forgiveness of sin through faith in Christ crucified upon the cross. This was the message that Paul declared he was ready to preach at Rome, the great heart of the world. It was not the world's wisdom that he would proclaim there, but Christ crucified.

I am not ashamed of the *remedy* of the gospel for the sins of the world. Paul said that he was not ashamed of the gospel because therein was revealed the righteousness of God—the way in which God saves a sinner and bestows righteousness upon man. Rome had all kinds of power and all kinds of wisdom; but although the world shook beneath the march of its legions, it had no power "unto salvation." I might be ashamed of a religion that overlooked my transgression and my sin. I might be ashamed of some cheap forgiveness which compromised the righteousness and holiness of God. But never can I be ashamed of that sublime act and fact whereby God in Christ reconciles me unto Himself, and leaves me pardoned and justified, presents me faultless before the presence of His glory, so that even the greatest archangel in heaven dare not stand before me and say, "I accuse thee." I am not ashamed of the gospel that can take a poor, dying thief and make him fit for the company of paradise.

I am not ashamed of the *results* of the gospel. Some years ago I sailed into the harbor of Syracuse, and on the waterfront I saw the statue of Archimedes, the famous Greek engineer, who, at the Siege of Syracuse, set fire to the Roman fleet by the refraction of his mirrors. He was the man who said that if he could find a place on which to stand and rest his lever, he could move the world.

Two centuries after that, a ship came sailing into the bay of Syracuse from Malta, and on that ship was a prisoner in chains on his way to Rome. Yet he was the man who had the place on which to stand and had found the lever with which to move the world. The charge brought against him by the rioters at Thessalonica was in the highest sense true—"These that have turned the world upside down are come hither also" (Acts 17:6).

The gospel *did* turn the world upside down. Do not be misled or deceived by the Satanic outbursts of animalism and tyranny and human ferocity which curse and shadow our world today. In spite of all that, as compared with that hard pagan world into which the gospel first came, the world today is a world that has been turned upside down.

Is the world's labor done today by slaves? Is one half the population of the world slave? Are prisoners taken in battle put to the sword? Are little children exposed and left to die by their parents on the hillsides and in the forests? Is woman a plaything and chattel of mankind? Why is it that great church buildings are not centers of vice and prostitution, as many of the temples of the ancient world were? To ask these questions is to answer them. The power that wrought this great change was the gospel of Christ. Call up one by one the systems of darkness and tyranny and superstition which have darkened and cursed the earth, but which have long since disappeared; call them up out of their graves and ask them, "Who smote you? What made you pass?" And one by one they answer, "Christ smote us and we died."

I am not ashamed of the results of the gospel as manifested in its followers, the disciples of Jesus. This letter which Paul wrote to the Romans comes to a beautiful and touching conclusion with his personal greetings and salutations to the then humble, but now forever famous and immortal, disciples of Jesus in that great heart of the world: Mary, Andronicus, Junia, Amplias, Apelles, Herodion, the household of Narcissus, Rufus, Hermes. Paul was not ashamed of those disciples, and Christ was not ashamed of them.

We are not ashamed of the disciples of Jesus in our midst today. We can open the old family Bible and in the pages between the Old and the New Testament read the names of our own loved ones, names that are worthy to stand side by side with those Paul mentions in the end of his letter to the Romans, names which are written forever in the Lamb's Book of Life. No, we are not ashamed of them! Christ is not ashamed of them, and they shall walk with Him in white.

NOT ASHAMED OF THE GOSPEL'S HOPE FOR THE FUTURE

If it were a lost cause, instead of the only cause which shall conquer, we might be ashamed of it. But when we see the kingdoms and empires which have waxed and waned and disappeared, while the church goes on from age to age, we know that the gospel has in it the invincible power of God. Christ alone belongs to the ages.

We are not ashamed of the hope the gospel gives us that a new heaven and a new earth will succeed this present clouded scene of turmoil and strife and anguish and sin and suffering and woe. We watch the parade of all the kingdoms, all the rulers, and all the statesmen, and we realize anew that it is Christ alone who stands in the midst of the seven golden candlesticks, He that lives and was dead, and, behold, is alive forevermore, who has the keys of authority, and will one day right all wrongs and solve all problems, and out of the present chaos and war and strife and injustice, bring in everlasting peace.

When we think of Him, we behold heaven opened and the white horse and his rider going forth to conquer. We are not ashamed of the fact that by the power of the gospel the blessed age one day will come, and heaven and earth shall ring with the shout, "Alleluiah: for the Lord God omnipotent reigneth. . . . The kingdoms of this world are become the kingdoms of our Lord, and of his Christ" (Rev. 19:6).

I am not ashamed of the gospel's hope for you and for me, as individuals. When we measure man by time, by the incidents and events of this world, what is he but an insect that spreads his wings for a brief moment and then is gone forever? But when we measure man by the gospel, by redemption, by the fact that in Christ man is called to honor and glory and immortality, then "what a piece of work is a man!"

We cannot make light of death, or its universal reign.

> There is no armor against Fate;
>> Death lays his icy hand on kings:
>>> Scepter and crown
>>> Must tumble down,
>> And in the dust be equal made
>> With the poor crooked scythe and spade.

I know the guesses, the surmises, the perhapses of the philosophers, what the Platos and the Ciceros and the Socrates' have said on the subject, and I know how cold they leave the heart. When I hear what they have to say, then I am not ashamed of Christ, who said, not, "I think there is another life," or, "I hope there is," or, "There ought to be," or, "There may be," but, "I *am* the resurrection, and the life."

> To Him I owe my life and breath,
>> And all the joys I have;
> He makes me triumph over death
>> He saves me from the grave.

The gospel of Christ is still the power of God unto salvation. But there is one condition upon which it bestows its power. It is the power of God unto salvation *to everyone that believeth.* This mightiest power on earth is nothing to you or for you until you believe. To as many as receive Christ, to everyone who believes, He gives power to become the sons of God. What about your life as a Christian? Is there little in it to suggest that the gospel which you profess has power in it? Is it having little power over your pocketbook, your business, your passions, your family relationships, little power to help you in the time of sorrow and trouble and temptation? Then let your prayer be, "Lord, increase my faith." According to our faith in the gospel, so will its power be in our lives.

And now to you who have never confessed the name of Christ,

and have never been ashamed of the gospel because you have never believed it: Even the greatest angel in heaven could not compel your faith, but all the angels in heaven rejoice over you when you believe and repent. All that the gospel did for Paul or anyone else—it can do for you and me if we fulfill its one condition, and that is that you believe. "If thou shalt confess with thy mouth the Lord Jesus, and shalt believe in thine heart that God hath raised him from the dead, thou shalt be saved" (Rom. 10:9). And what it means to be saved, what it means for a man made in the image of God to be restored to the divine likeness, what it means to unfold and expand all the powers of your soul, it will take the measureless love of God, the priceless blood of Christ, the endless years of eternity, and all the music of all the angels of heaven to describe and tell.

7

ALL THINGS WORK TOGETHER FOR GOOD

And we know that all things work together for
good to them that love God (Romans 8:28).

In the conclusion of his great book *Tess of the d'Urbervilles*, Thomas Hardy describes the ending of the life of that unfortunate young woman. She had slain the man who had seduced her, and, judged guilty by the law, was to be hanged at eight in the morning. Her husband, Angel Clare, and her sister stand outside the walls of the grim penitentiary, waiting for the hour to strike. Their eyes are fixed on the flagstaff of the tower. Presently the clock strikes the hour of eight. Slowly a black flag goes up on the flagstaff, and then comes down. Knowing what that means, Angel Clare and his companion kneel on the ground as if in prayer. Hardy brings the scene to a close with this sentence: "'Justice' was done, and the President of the Immortals, in Aeschylean phrase, had ended his sport with Tess."

That is one view of life and of what happens to us in this life and how it happens. We are just the sport of the grim and inscrutable President of the Universe. We are the playthings of fate and of chance.

But there is another view of life, and of what happens to us in this life. We have it here in these words of Paul, where he says that we are in the hands of a wise and beneficent God, who has a deep interest in our lives and arranges and rules the events of our life so that all things work together for our final good.

"All things work together for good to them that love God." No verse in the Bible claims more than that, covers more territory, offers more hope and comfort. If what this verse says is so, then every cloud has its silver lining of hope, and every event in our life is capable of producing final and lasting good to our souls. Men hear that verse, and at once there are different reactions. One asks, "Can it be true?" Another says, "I know it is not true; the experience of life is against it." And another, "I could wish that it were true." And another, "I hope that it is true." But there are some who are able to say with Paul, "We know that all things work together for good to them that love God."

Those words "I know," "we know," were favorites with Paul. He says to the Philippians, speaking of his trial and imprisonment, "I know that this shall turn to my salvation through your prayer" (Phil. 1:19). Again, speaking of the future life, he says, "We know that if our earthly house of this tabernacle were dissolved, we have a building of God, an house not made with hands, eternal in the heavens" (2 Cor. 5:1). And most familiar, perhaps, of all, "I know whom I have believed, and am persuaded that he is able to keep that which I have committed unto him against that day" (2 Tim. 2:12). In Romans 8:28 we have another great "I know": "We know that all things work together for good to them that love God."

How did Paul know that this was so? Was it by a process of logic or demonstration? When he was caught up into the third heaven and heard things such as it was not lawful for him to utter, was he given an apocalypse of the final fate and lot of all those who have loved and trusted God? In none of these ways could he have known the truth of what he asserts in this verse, when he says here, "we know that all things work together for good." It is the conviction, the inner feeling of certainty, the knowledge that is born of faith. "The heart," Pascal used to say, "has reasons of which the mind knows nothing." And in this great passage Paul is dealing with the experience and the faith of a loving Christian heart.

Whether what Paul says is true or not, all will acknowledge a great difference between being in the hands of a grim and speechless fate and being in the hands of a loving God. When I am glad, when I am sad, when I am strong, when I am weak, when I am successful, when I am beaten, is it just a happenstance, without any meaning or purpose? Or, in the hands of a loving God, are all things working together for my good? It would be impossible to measure the gulf that is fixed between those two theories of life.

This verse is the gateway to the sublime and mysterious temple of foreordination and predestination, as that truth is declared here in this famous passage in Romans. But here, introducing it, is the practical result of faith in such a foreordaining and predestinating God, and that result is the confidence that, loving and trusting Him, all things are working together for our good. Men have raised objections to the doctrine of predestination, but always on the negative side, upon which Paul does not touch in this passage. But whatever objections men might have to the doctrine of predestination, as a doctrine, certainly they could have no objection to the result of believing such a doctrine, if the result is that "all things work together for good to them that love God."

WHAT PAUL DOES NOT SAY HERE

In the first place, this verse is not a statement of God's dealings with men in general. That we have elsewhere in the Bible, but not here. Here we have His dealings with God's people, with those who love and trust and obey Him.

Yet Paul does not say here that all things are good, for he and those to whom he was writing, and we today, know that it is not so. There is much in the world that is not good: hard labor that produces nothing, disappointed hopes, pain, sorrow, and heartache. These are not good. Hatred, persecution, defeat, none of these things, in themselves, are good; and none of these things, by and of themselves, are capable of producing good. And Paul does not say that they are. Neither does Paul say here that all things, of themselves, can and do produce good, for often they do not. Neither does he say that all things, working together, produce good to all, regardless of the character or the faith or the love in those to whom these things happen. What he does say is that all things work together for good, for the good of the soul, to all those who have responded to God's call and love God and put their trust in Him.

"To Them That Love God"

In this verse are two important facts—God's wise and beautiful plan, and man's response to and cooperation with that plan. We begin, therefore, at the end of this verse, "to them that love God." Who are the people in whom all the events of life produce lasting good? They are those who, called of God, respond to His call with love and obedience, and trust God for His plan in their lives.

All kinds of things happen to all kinds of people. There is a lofty impartiality in the general providence of life. That was what made the sage of Ecclesiastes say, "I myself perceived also that one event happeneth to them all" (2:4). God makes His sun to shine and His rains to descend upon the good and evil, the just and the unjust. The Old Testament saints seemed to have been troubled sometimes about the prosperity of the wicked. But take it by and large, the same general run of events happen to all kinds of people. All know sickness, sorrow, losses, failures, and disappointments. But although the same kind of things happen to all people, the results are not the same. The same rain descended, the same floods came, the same winds blew and beat upon the two houses, but the end was not the same. One house fell; the other stood secure.

When Paul said all things work together for good, he was thinking, of course, of the hardships and adversities to which he and those Roman Christians were subjected. Adversity is said to have sweet uses, and, like the toad, to carry a jewel in its head. But this is not necessarily or inevitably so. In many cases adversity hardens, blasts, embitters. You might prune year after year the vine of a poison ivy, and yet year after year it would still produce poison. So the pruning knife of adversity in itself can produce no good in the life of man.

All depends upon how the soul reacts to adversity, to what the world calls misfortune. This is fully stated elsewhere by the writer, where he says that "No chastening for the present seemeth to be joyous, but grievous: nevertheless afterward it yieldeth the peaceable fruit of righteousness unto them which are exercised thereby" (Heb. 12:11). That "afterward," no doubt, takes in not only a space of time after the immediate chastening or affliction, but the final and full fruit of affliction received in love and trust in the life to come.

"ALL THINGS"

When a man hears this verse, his mind at once settles upon the word "all." Had Paul said "a few things" or "some things," no one would have been disposed to question. But he said "all things."

You say, "I believe in God," "I believe in the providence of God." Are you sure that you do? The test of belief in God and His providence comes when He sends us hard things. It is significant and encouraging too that these words were uttered by no fair-weather soldier, but by a scarred and veteran warrior for Christ who could point to the marks in his body that he bore for Christ's sake. In one of his letters he gives us the extraordinary catalogue of the woes he had endured—hunger, thirst, loneliness, sickness, prison, robberies, scourging, shipwreck (2 Cor. 11:23-25)—and yet Paul never reproaches God, never complains that his life has been a hard one. On the contrary, he says that he is able to rejoice in all these things because he knows that they are working out good in him and for him.

In his letter to the Philippians, Paul says that the "things which happened unto me have fallen out rather unto the furtherance of the gospel" (1:12). What were these things that had happened to him in recent months? Mobbing and near destruction by the fanatics of Jerusalem; a plot to assassinate him; shipwreck in the Mediterranean; the hard march to Rome from Naples; the prison; the rough soldiers; the trial before the brutal Nero. In all those things there was nothing that was in itself "good." But he could say, looking back, that all these things had worked good because they had given him an opportunity to preach the gospel. It is not hard to say that all things, minus the hard things, work together for good, but it shows real faith in providence when we can say that *all* things, even the hard things, work together for good.

Some years ago the whole country was horrified by the kidnapping and murder of the son of a physician in Seattle. After many days the boy's naked body was found in the northern snows. The perpetrator of the crime was never discovered and never punished, unless by his own conscience. But the father of the boy, in a statement to the public at that time, said that he was a Christian, and he believed that even in an event such as this there was a wise and a kind providence at work. There even the hard thing, the terrible thing, was working good because of the reaction of a heart that loved and trusted God.

"ALL THINGS WORK TOGETHER"

That word "together" is one of the most important of all in this great promise. Paul does not say that everything works good by itself, even to all those who love God. But he says that all things together work good—one event before another, after another, with another, combined with other events. The different and varied events of a military campaign must not be judged by themselves, but in their relationship to the general strategy and to the final victory. You cannot judge a military campaign by separated and isolated events and episodes, such as torpedoed ships, forts attacked and taken, reverses, lives lost, cities fallen. All must be related to the end. And so it is with the events in the lives of those who love God. They must be related to the grand strategy which God is working out in human life. Looking back on the different events in his life that had fitted one into another, many of which had been terrible events, but which had now brought him to his present state of deliverance, Robinson Crusoe remarked, "How strange a checkerboard of providence is the life of man!"

That plan of God for man's life must embrace not only this life, but that which is to come. So when Paul says here that all things work together for good, although indirect, it is one of the most powerful declarations on the subject of the future life. For if everyone were sure that life ended with this life, no one would have the slightest interest in what Paul says about all things working together for good. The falsity of such a statement would be manifest at once.

This verse of Paul states the only theory of life that can stand the test of the facts of life—the purpose of life is to produce good (moral and spiritual good) with a view to its reward and complete liberation in the life to come. So far as the demonstration is concerned, it will indeed take the other life to prove that all things work together for good. "In that day," said Christ, "ye shall ask me nothing" (John 16:23). Both men and angels will be satisfied with the end, with the good that has been produced, and men and angels shall echo the verdict that was pronounced at the end of the first Creation, "It was very good."

CONCLUSION

The practical question is not a discussion or a debate as to the government of life and how its events are arranged, but what is life doing for you? Is it working good in you? If there is something in your life which you know cannot be changed, do you have the faith that it is working good? In other words, are you loving and trusting God? Are you responding to His purpose in every event of your life? Then, if so, you can say, even to David, "David, put down thy harp for a moment, and let me too sing that great music, 'My times are in thy hand.'" And even to great Paul himself you can say, "Paul, be silent for a moment and let me pronounce thy great conviction, 'I know that all things work together for good to them that love God.'"

8

A HOUSE NOT MADE WITH HANDS

For we know that if our earthly house of this tabernacle were dissolved,
we have a building of God, an house not made with hands,
eternal in the heavens   (2 Corinthians 5:1).

In the far-famed Santa Clara Valley in California, not far from San Jose, there stands in the midst of a great orchard what is said to be the largest house in the world. It was built, or started, in the 1890s by a Mrs. Winchester. At first only a pleasing country home of ordinary dimensions, it has been altered and added to, until today it covers, with its outbuildings, a space of fourteen acres. Adding apartment after apartment, room after room, and chamber after chamber, the owner became obsessed with the idea of building statelier mansions. Today the house is a curious and amazing labyrinth of winding stairways, upside-down pillars and posts, blind doors, intricate passages, and hundreds of windows. If left in one of the interior rooms, the visitor would have a hard time finding his way out of the labyrinth. As the owner added room to room and chamber to chamber, she labored under the obsession that as long as she kept building and adding, she herself would not die. But at length Death came, Death which is no respecter of houses. Death came and found its way up the strange stairways and through the many passages to the blue room where she lay.

That is the fate of all earthly houses, whether the largest in the world or the meanest shanty. One day it is dissolved, destroyed, taken down. It is not otherwise with the tabernacle which we inhabit in this stage of our life, the body. Death, the great dissolver, takes it down.

PAUL'S HEAVENLY VISION

Only one man in the Bible ever got into heaven and came back again to earth. That man was Paul, who was caught up, he tells us, into the third heaven. Yet he distinctly tells us that he was not permitted to utter what he had seen or heard. How wonderful that would be, if we could read what Paul saw and heard in heaven! It would answer many questions and put an end to many speculations. At the same time it is Paul who tells us, more than any other in the Bible, about the nature of the heavenly life. He starts off by saying, "We know that . . . we have a building of God, an house not made with hands." He was not speaking from any kind of natural knowledge or human experience. In his famous speech by the grave of a child, Robert Ingersoll, the well-known agnostic, said:

"We do not know which is the greatest blessing, life or death. We cannot say that death is not good. We do not know whether the grave is the end of life, or the door of another, or whether the night here is not somewhere else a dawn. . . . Every cradle asks us, Whence? and every coffin, Whither? The poor barbarian weeping above his dead can answer the question as intelligently and satisfactorily as the robed priest of the most authentic creed. The tearful ignorance of the one is just as consoling as the learned and unmeaning words of the other."

So far as natural knowledge is concerned, what Ingersoll said is so. No one, in that sense, knows anything about the life to come. But Paul is speaking in the light of divine inspiration, in the light of who Christ is and what He has done. On that ground and in that light he says, "We know that . . . we have a building from God, an house not made with hands."

Paul did not wish to die any more than anyone else. In his "Elegy Written in a Country Churchyard," Thomas Gray wrote:

> For who, to dumb Forgetfulness a prey,
> This pleasing, anxious being e'er resigned,
> Left the warm precincts of the cheerful day,
> Nor cast one longing, ling'ring look behind?

Paul had hoped to forestall death by living until Christ came. That is what he refers to when in another passage he says, speaking of the coming of the Lord, "We shall not all sleep, but we shall all be changed" (1 Cor. 15:51). And again in his First Epistle to the Thessalonians, where he says that when Christ comes again, "We which are alive and remain shall be caught up together with them"—that is, the dead who have been raised—"in the clouds, to meet the Lord in the air" (4:17). That was the great expectation entertained by the disciples of Paul's day. And it is a great possibility for believers today.

Yet Paul contemplates the alternative, that he will have to leave this earthly scene through the gateway of the dead. In the passage just before this, from which we take our text, it would seem that Paul is expecting death. There is no doubt that he is feeling the inroads of mortality. He says that death is working in him. His outward man is perishing, his soul's dark cottage, battered and decayed, was letting in new light through chinks that time had made. Yet the contemplation of mortality, of death, if that is God's will for him, in no way dims his hope. Though his outer man is perishing, his inner man is being renewed, growing stronger, for he is not bound by the seen and the temporal, but looks ever at the things which are not seen, and eternal. In a few luminous sentences he proceeds to set forth his hopes, the great certainty for all believers.

A MIXTURE OF METAPHORS

If you are a Plato or a Paul, you have the liberty to mix your metaphors, and here Paul mixes his metaphors, but in a grand way. He likens the change from this mortal body to the heavenly body, first of all, to putting off an old garment and being clothed with a new garment, the heavenly garment. But we fix our thought now on this metaphor of the tabernacle, the tent, and the house not made of hands. Although there were many splendid houses in that day, multitudes of people, then as now, dwelt in tents. The tent could be taken down and the place of habitation changed. This was a very natural metaphor for Paul, because that was his trade and profession. And in this very city, to whose church he was writing, Paul had worked at his trade as a tent maker, living with Aquila and Priscilla, who were of the same craft. You see then how natural it was for him to employ this metaphor about the tent.

He says, "If our earthly house of this tabernacle, [or tent,] were dissolved, we have a building from God." Literally, he is saying, if the earthly tent were taken down, unloosed, as one takes down a tent by loosening its ropes. So in the book of Job, we have that metaphor for death, "Is not their tent-cord plucked up within them?" (Job 4:21 ASV). So at death the cords of the earthly tents are loosened; the tabernacle, the body, comes down. But when that happens, the soul moves out into its building of God, the house not made with hands. Paul is thinking here not so much of heaven as a place, as when Christ spoke of the house of many mansions, but of our life in that place, the kind of house and body in which the soul will dwell there. So he says elsewhere, "We have borne the image of the earthy, we shall also bear the image of the heavenly" (1 Cor. 15:49).

In this body, in this earthy tent, the apostle says, we groan. The reference seems to be to the burdens, sicknesses, diseases of the body—all those ills of which everyone knows the flesh is heir. But in that other body, not the tent, but our house not made with hands, there will be no frustration, no weakness, no groaning, no sinning, and no dying. A tent is frail. The wind can sweep it over. A tent, even if Paul had made it with his careful hands, could last only for a few years, and those who live in it are subjected to many discomforts and trials. But the heavenly house, the one not made with hands, is strong, abiding, enduring, incorruptible, fading not away, ever bestowing great blessing upon those who live in it.

Contrasting the life here in the body, in the tent, the apostle says that he longs to get into that other house: "Whilst we are at home in the body, we are absent from the Lord" (2 Cor. 5:6). Therefore he is glad and willing to be absent from the body, to move out of the tent and into the house not made with hands so that he can be at home with the Lord. That did not mean, of course, that in this life, dwelling in the tent, a believer does not have the presence and the comfort of Christ, for no one knew that comfort and presence better than Paul. But he looks forward to the consummation of our Christian life, when we shall no longer walk by faith as we must now, but by sight, and shall be ever with the Lord.

That thought, how in the body, the tent, we are absent from the Lord, and how in the heavenly house we are at home with the Lord, is summed up in a stanza of a poem by the Scottish poet James Montgomery. A finer than this was hardly ever written:

> Here in the body pent,
>   Absent from Him I roam,
> Yet nightly pitch my moving tent
>   A day's march nearer home.

No one can lead the strong victorious Christian life, or do the real work of a believer in Christ in this world, unless he entertains this certain hope that Paul did; unless, when confronted by the vicissitudes and dangers and ultimate mortality in this life, casting its shadow over all that we do and attempt, he can say, "I know that when this earthly tent is dissolved, taken down, I have a building from God, an house not made with hands." If he entertains that hope, then he can say to himself, concerning life's work and life's most sacred and tender hopes, "We know that our labor is not in vain in the Lord" (1 Cor. 15:58).

We might wish, when our longing thoughts go out toward the heavenly world, that Paul had gone a little further than this and told us more about the nature of that body and the house which is to be ours in the Kingdom of the redeemed. But he does throw out one very luminous sentence on this subject when he says elsewhere that "as we have borne the image of the earthy, we shall also bear the image of the heavenly" (1 Cor. 15:49). The image of the earthy, the body, the tent in which we live here, was well adapted to its life and its needs. And so will be the image of the heavenly, the house not made with hands. What will the image of the heavenly be like?

> How will the change strike me and you
> In the house not made with hands?

IMAGES OF THE HEAVENLY

We know that that image of the heavenly will be the image of power and strength. It is sown in weakness, this body, Paul says, at death; but it will be raised in power. Even here in this tent in which we groan, living under the limitations of time and sense and under the shadow of sin, what a marvelous instrument the body is. How quickly, how perfectly it expresses the thought of the mind, the feeling of the heart, and the aspiration of the soul. If that is so even here, then what will it be like when this mortal has put on immortality, when the redeemed body has been reunited to the redeemed soul and man has been restored to what God had in mind at the beginning, when He said, "Let us make man in our own image" (Gen. 1:26)?

The image of the heavenly will be the image of the holy. The shadow of sin will be lifted, and man, clothed and in his right mind, will desire what God wills for him, and rejoice in his salvation. If Jesus said that the angels of heaven rejoice over one sinner who repents, it is well to remember that they rejoice not only over what man has been saved *from*, but over what he has been restored *to*, the lost image of God.

The image of the heavenly, we are sure, will be the image of great enterprise, of great service. They shall go from strength to strength. What that will be we must leave to the imagination. Yet we can be certain that Elijah, since he was taken to heaven in a whirlwind, and David, since he laid by his harp, and Isaiah and Paul, since they ceased to preach, have not been left unemployed, but find even greater work to do there than they did here.

The image of the heavenly will be the image of great joy. Man was created for joy. The morning star sang together and all the sons of God shouted for joy when man was born. One of those joys of heaven will be to see and talk with the great personalities of time and of eternity. In the *Essay on Old Age*, which Cicero wrote at the time of his poignant grief over the death of his beloved daughter Tullia, he says that if after death, and on his way to Elysium, some superior being should meet him in his flight and make him the offer of returning again to his body, he would without hesitation reject the offer, so much would he prefer going into Elysium to be with Socrates and Plato and all the ancient worthies, and to spend his time in converse with them.

If even a pagan could feel that way, then how ought a Christian to feel when he contemplates the joy of conversing with Moses and Samuel and David and Isaiah and Peter and John and Paul! But greater still will be the joy of conversing with those whom we have loved long since and lost awhile. And highest of all, the joy of being "at home with the Lord," whom having not seen, we love.

FROM DEATH TO LIFE

The New Testament employs at least five different metaphors when it speaks of the change from death to life. It calls it an "exodus." The children of Israel made their exodus out of Egypt. So for the believer death is an exodus from the bondage of time to the joy and liberty of the sons of God. It speaks too of death as a "sleep." We shall not all sleep. As one awakens out of the sleep of the night, refreshed and ready for the new day, so out of death's slumber, we awaken to be satisfied with the likeness of God.

Again it speaks of death as the "sailing," or the unmooring of the ship. That was the way Paul put it when he was just on the margin of the other world. He said, "The time of my departure," literally the *analusis*, the unmooring of the ship, has come. As the ship weighs anchor, hoists the sail, and starts off toward the unseen and yet certain port beyond the horizon, so at death the believer weighs anchor and sails for the eternal haven.

And here is another metaphor: *the tent is struck*. We move out of the earthly tent and enter into our eternal house, a house not made with hands. And last of all there is that metaphor most dear to our hearts, the metaphor of home. That was the one employed by Jesus. "In my Father's house are many mansions. . . I go to prepare a place for you, . . . that where I am there ye may be also" (John 14:2). So Christ and His great apostle sing the same song. To be there will be to be at home with the Lord.

Can you say with Paul: "I know that I have a building of God, a house not made with hands, eternal in the heavens"? Or is your sole possession just what you have here in this life, in this world, the frail tent soon to be dissolved and smitten down by the winds of death? Are you living, as Paul said he endeavored to live, that you might be acceptable to God, "for we shall all stand before the judgment seat of Christ"?

When we get to heaven there is one thing certain: We shall say, "The half hath never yet been told!" And this too is certain, as John Newton said in his great hymn:

> When we've been there ten thousand years,
> > Bright shining as the sun,
> We've no less days to sing His praise
> > Than when we first begun.

9

CHRIST RECONCILING THE WORLD

God was in Christ, reconciling the world unto himself. . . . For he hath made him to be sin for us, who knew no sin (2 Corinthians 5:19-21).

If it is not so, then let us close the Bible, mute the organ, empty the pews, silence the hymns, lock the doors of the church, and throw the key into the river; for we have nothing to talk about, nothing to sing about and nothing upon which to build our hopes. But since it is true—that "God was in Christ, reconciling the world unto himself"—we have something to talk about, something to sing about, and a solid foundation upon which to build the structure of our everlasting hope.

The Atonement is God's own mystery. The best that we can do is to stretch forth humble hands of faith and touch the outermost fringe of its crimson garment. The cherubim and the seraphim cover the rest with their wings.

The world's storms which are abroad drive the church back to the cardinal truths and mountainous facts, the grand particularities of the Christian faith. And here is the grandest of them all, the one that takes in all the others, that "God was in Christ, reconciling the world unto himself."

We are glad that the Atonement is greater than man's mind, for could I measure it with the measure of my finite mind, then it would not be great enough and deep enough for the needs of my infinite heart. The cross is a truth that we can not know and yet know. If that seems a paradox, it is an inspired paradox, for that is what Paul says of the cross, of the gospel of reconciliation. He prays that his friends may know the length and the breadth and the depth and the height of it and, he adds, "know the love of Christ, which passeth knowledge" (Eph. 3:19). There you are—you both know it and cannot know it. You cannot know it with the mind, but you can know it and receive it and rejoice in it, and trust in it with your heart. This is the truth that is the chief part of our salvation, the anchor of our faith, and the refuge of our hope. Let us look, then, at Paul's great statement of the Atonement—perhaps, for our understanding and our needs, the most satisfactory in the Bible.

"GOD WAS IN CHRIST"

If Christ offers Himself as our Savior and Redeemer, and commands our loyalty and obedience as our Master, then this is the first thing we want to know about Him: Who is He?

It was the first thing Paul wanted to know about Him. When for the first time he came into actual contact with Christ, that was what he asked, "Who art thou, Lord?" Now he knows. After all his remarkable and rich experience Paul knows who Christ is, and this is the way he puts it: "God was in Christ reconciling the world unto himself."

It is always appropriate and always important that we should emphasize the real and tender humanity of our Lord. But the church must always lift up and exalt the glorious deity of her Lord. Always over His head is the halo of transcendent miracle, for in Him dwelt the fulness of the Godhead bodily. We do not say that in Christ there was a nobler soul than ever inhabited man. We do not say that He was more filled with the Holy Spirit than any other man. We do not say that He, more than any other, revealed the holiness and the goodness of God. But what we do say is that God was in Christ, so that when Christ came into the world, it was God who came, when Christ spake and taught in parables, it was God who spake and taught, when Christ paused by the wayside and touched the sores of the leper or the eyes of the blind, it was God who touched them, and when Christ died on the cross, it was God who died. In the mere story of the unmerited death of a beautiful life on the cursed tree—how with a heart full of love He was put to cruel death by wicked men—in that there is no gospel. It may be moving, pathetic, appealing, but there is no gospel, no message in it. But there is a gospel in the fact that "God was in Christ, reconciling the world unto himself." This is the Christ of the Old Testament, the Christ of the New Testament, the Christ of the patriarchs and the prophets, of the apostles and the martyrs, of the angels and the archangels, the Christ of the ages.

"RECONCILING THE WORLD TO HIMSELF"

God was in Christ. But what did He come to do? Why did Christ come? The question has sometimes been asked: Would there have been an incarnation of God in Christ even if man had not sinned and fallen? Conceivably, to man in a state of innocence, there might have come some fuller revelation and manifestation of God His Creator. But such an incarnation would have been altogether different from the historic incarnation. What we know is that Christ came into the world in view of man's sin. He came to redeem, He came to save, He came to reconcile. "This is a faithful saying, and worthy of all acceptation, that Christ Jesus came into the world to save sinners" (1 Tim. 1:15).

If Christ came to reconcile the world to God, then there must be a state of separation, alienation, and estrangement. One would not speak of reconciling two loyal and trusting friends; one would not speak of reconciling two casual acquaintances; one would not speak of reconciling a man in San Francisco and a man in New York who had never seen one another. But one does speak of reconciling a father and son who have become estranged, a mother and a daughter who have become alienated, a husband and a wife who have become separated.

Reconciliation can take place only between parties who have had close relationship one with another, and that is true of man in his relationship to God. Man ever has to do with God. No sinning, no wandering, no rebellion can break the eternal tie of his relationship with God. Fallen, stained, and rebellious though he may be, he is by creation a member of God's family. This, then, is the condition which exists between God and man. As Isaiah expresses it: "Your iniquities have separated between you and your God, and your sins have hid his face from you" (Isa. 59:2).

If man needs to be reconciled to God because he is alienated and separated from God, where are the evidences of such alienation and enmity? One of the striking proofs is found in man's religious history. By that I mean the history of false religions. There we have a whole vast system of rites and sacrifices and vain libations, a vast effort of man to appease God and to reconcile God to man. But the Gospel, the cross, is the story of how God reconciles man to himself. Yet this profound and pathetic blunder of false religions is in itself a striking evidence of the fact that man has recognized that there is something out of place, something wrong in his relationship to God.

Another powerful witness to the need of reconciliation, to the fact of separation, is the state of the world. To ask where the signs of man's rebellion and separation from the mind of God are, is like taking a man down to the Point in Pittsburgh and asking him where the rivers are.

All one has to do is to take up the morning paper, or listen for half an hour to the news that comes over the radio and television, to learn the sad state of the world and human nature. As in Isaiah's time, the world is a chaos, unable to rest, ever casting up the mire and dirt of its sin, its crimes and its folly. Look over the world of the last few years and what do you see? Flames of battle and billows of smoke rising toward heaven; rivers of blood flowing everywhere through the nations—rivers of blood quenching and drowning the ambitions, the expectations, the hopes, the loves, and the joys of untold millions of people.

Alas, what a world it is! Everywhere one hears the deep undertone of its sorrow and its woe. The Welsh have a tradition that once the Almighty held a great review of all the worlds of the far-flung universe. One by one the stars and the planets and the satellites passed by in review, and as each passed the eternal Father smiled upon them. But when the earth passed God blushed. Yes, sin is the one great human calamity, as universal as human nature, as eternal as human history.

But there is a yet more striking evidence for the necessity of reconciliation with God. No man ever felt his need of Christ as

Savior because of the sad and lamentable state of the world. No one ever felt his need of Christ as Savior because he visited the deserted temples and fallen altars of the pagan faiths, where men sought to propitiate the deity and reconcile God to man.

The only time man feels the need of Christ as Savior is when he looks within his own heart. Is not every man who breathes an evidence to himself, if not to others, of his need of reconciliation with God? Is all right within? Are there no whispers of accusation? Are there no shadows of transgression? Must you not often say, as Paul, the great battler, said, "The good that I would I do not: but the evil which I would not, that I do"? Are there no old wounds that reopen when you come to the Communion Table? And if perchance you have been guarded and delivered from certain gross transgressions and sins, what about the greatest sin of all, the sin of self-righteousness?

In "The Minister's Black Veil," a powerful parable of life, Nathaniel Hawthorne tells of a New England minister who appeared for the first time before his congregation with a black veil over his face. Some thought that he had gone mad, and others that it was a token of remorse and sorrow for past transgression. All through the services the mysterious veil was never once withdrawn. It shook with his measured breath as he gave out the psalm, and threw its obscurity between him and the holy page as he read the Scriptures. The next Sabbath it was the same, and so on through all the Sabbaths, and through all the years of a long ministry, until the minister's summons came and he lay upon his deathbed. A neighboring minister who had come in to pray with him besought him, before the veil of eternity should be lifted, to cast the black veil from his face. At that the dying minister raised himself on his pillow and exclaimed:

"Why do you tremble at me alone? Tremble also at each other! Have men avoided me, and women shown no pity, and children screamed and fled, only for my black veil? What, but the mystery which it obscurely typifies, has made this piece of crape so awful? When the friend shows his inmost heart to his friend; the lover to his best beloved; when man does not vainly shrink from the eye of his Creator, loathsomely treasuring up the secret of his sin; then deem me a monster, for the symbol beneath which I have lived, and die! I look around me, and, lo! on every visage A Black Veil!"

Yes; if Christ came to reconcile, He came to do what the world needs most of all. And if we had a world reconciled now to God, all men so reconciled, then the cannon's lips would grow still, the clouds of battle would lift, social injustice would disappear, time would run back and fetch the age of gold, and the stars that sang together over man's creation would sing again over his restoration.

"HE HATH MADE HIM TO BE SIN FOR US, WHO KNEW NO SIN"

We have seen that "God was in Christ, reconciling the world unto himself." But how did He do it? How could it be done? Here on one side is man, a member of God's family by divine creation, but alienated, stained, rebellious, guilty, and sully. And here on the other side is God, infinitely holy, infinitely just, and infinitely merciful. How then can God and man be brought together? How can this gulf between God and man be bridged? How will God deal with sin? One answer might be, indeed often is: Let Him overlook and disregard the sin of man. Let Him forgive man without any regard for the state of his soul, or for what is due to God's holiness and justness.

That was the plan David followed when his heart yearned to go out to the banished Absalom, banished for the murder of his brother. He brought Absalom home again, but without any change in Absalom's heart, without any due recognition of Absalom's great offense; and the result was that Absalom proceeded to greater and more infamous crimes.

Another might say: If man has sinned, if he has broken the holy law of God, then let him bear the consequence of his sin.

But God, who is just, is also infinitely good and merciful. How can He deal with man, the sinner? How can He show the mind of God toward sin and yet restore and forgive and reconcile man? It was indeed a problem for a god to solve, and He solved it like a god, solved it in that majestic and sublime act of His justice and His mercy, whereby, when the sun hid His face and the earth reeled and the graves were opened, Christ, the Son of God, died for us on the cross. There God upheld the majesty and holiness of His nature and His law, and at the same time opened the gate of repentance and forgiveness for mankind. He made Him who knew no sin, the holy and spotless Son of God, to be sin on our behalf.

God remained just, and yet the justifier of them that believe in Jesus. There on the cross mercy and truth are met together, righteousness and peace have kissed each other. Men say it would not be right for an innocent man to bear the penalties of a guilty man. God says it is not only right, but the foundation of all righteousness. Men say it would not be possible, even if one should desire to do so, for the innocent one to take the place of the guilty one. God says, "It is done." "For scarcely for a righteous man will one die: yet peradventure for a good man some would even dare to die. But God commendeth his love toward us, in that, while we were yet sinners, Christ died for us."

Here is the center of our Christian faith; here converge all the rites, and types and prophecies, all the songs and hopes and expectations, all the future glories of the life to come. The cross is the eternal fact. The cross is the eternal fact looking backward; for the cross was not an afterthought of God, but His eternal plan, and Christ, the Lamb of God, was slain from the foundation of the world. The cross is the eternal fact looking forward; for when John opens for us a window into heaven, that is what we see, the Lamb upon His throne, and that is what we hear, the music of the redeemed, singing their song and hymn "unto him that loved us, and washed us from our sins in his own blood."

"God was in Christ, reconciling the world unto himself." But if so, what about the world today? Where do we see the least sign of such reconciliation? I see it in the heart and life of every humble and sincere believer and follower of Christ who has put His trust in Him for redemption, and who follows in His steps. As for the world, and as for the future, we leave that to God. The great foundation has been laid, and one day the structure, the glorious temple of reconciliation, will be completed, and He who on the cross out of the darkness of the ninth hour cried, "It is finished," will one day from the throne of a reconciled universe cry out again, as John heard Him and saw Him, with all heaven and earth joining in that cry, "It is done!"

This then is the reconciliation of God in Christ, and this is our message and our only message, the ministry of reconciliation. You can never think too often about it, or rejoice too greatly in it.

Always there is occasion for us to go deeper, to ask ourselves questions like these: I have accepted the forgiveness and reconciliation of God in Christ, but does my life show that I have? Is there in me any thought, any ambition, any desire, any public or secret habit, any attitude or relationship that is contrary to the will of God? If there is, then as Christ's ambassador, I beseech you, be ye reconciled unto God.

10

THE UNSEARCHABLE RICHES OF CHRIST

Unto me . . . is this grace given, that I should preach. . . the unsearchable riches of Christ (Ephesians 3:8).

On a visit once to the anthracite coal regions of Pennsylvania at a time when they were celebrating the one hundredth anniversary of anthracite mining, I inquired of one who was familiar with the mining operations if these great deposits of coal, laid down through incalculable aeons of time, showed any signs of exhaustion. I was surprised to learn that 100 years of mining had touched only the outermost fringe of those great deposits of coal.

For long ages now, countless believers have been taking out of the gospel the riches of Christ. The theologians, the poets, the painters, the sculptors, the statesmen, the social reformers—all of them have drawn on the riches which are in Christ. But still those riches are as rich as ever. Inexhaustible, unsearchable riches!

Men seek riches. There is nothing ancient about that. In itself, that searching has something good in it, in that it implies a desire for independence and for power. Men sought riches in the world of Paul's day. Here he compares, or contrasts, the riches of the gospel with the riches of the world. Paul, like every writer and speaker, had certain terms and phrases which he liked to use. One of these words is "riches," when he comes to speak of Christ and the gospel. As many as thirteen times in his letters he employs this word—for example: "the riches of his goodness"; "his riches in glory"; "riches of the full assurance. . . of the mystery . . . of Christ"; "the depth of the riches both of the wisdom and knowledge of God"; and here in our text, "the unsearchable riches of Christ."

Paul was a great writer and a great speaker, but when he comes to write or speak of the gospel of Christ, he feels the limitation of words. After he has said all he can about the gift of God's love in Christ, he sums it all up by calling it "his *unspeakable* gift." In this same chapter from which we take our text he talks about knowing the length and the breadth and the depth and the height of the love of Christ, and then declares that it "passeth knowledge"—that it is unknowable.

When he holds out before believers in Christ the great victory that is possible for them, he says that "we are more than conquerors." He is referring to the magnificent triumph of the Roman conqueror, the most splendid spectacle of the ancient world. But even "conqueror" is not enough for Paul. He is compelled to say "more than conquerors." Likewise, when he thinks of the riches of Christ in the gospel, he declares that they are unsearchable, not only that they represent a mystery of love and power and justice and mercy which can never be searched out completely or explained, but that they are inexhaustible. Let us, therefore, explore for a little, with the New Testament as our guide, and Christian experience as our confirmation, some of the "unsearchable riches of Christ."

THE RICHES OF CHRIST AS AN EXAMPLE

We sometimes hear the phrase "in his steps." The world's bestselling novel was written with that for a title 100 or more years ago. The author of that beautiful metaphor is Peter, who, in his First Epistle, speaking to persecuted and afflicted disciples of Christ, reminded them that Christ had suffered before they had, and for them. He then goes on to say how Christ is our example, not only in suffering, but in every field of life: "Leaving us an example, that ye should follow his steps: who did no sin, neither was guile found in his mouth: who, when he was reviled, reviled not again; when he suffered he threatened not; but committed himself to him that judgeth righteously" (1 Pet. 2:21). That was Peter's familiar and beautiful statement about Christ as our example, and how it is our duty and our privilege and honor to follow in His steps.

The phrase reminds us of another best-selling little book, one of the smallest ever written, but one of the most famous—perhaps, after the Bible itself, the most read of all books. Like incense it has "diffused itself down the aisles of the universal church." In times of sorrow and trouble the souls of men have found light and comfort and hope in its pages. The book commences with these words: "He that followeth me, walketh not in darkness, saith the Lord. These are the words of Christ, by which we are admonished, how we ought to imitate his life and manners." That is the beginning of *The Imitation of Christ*, by Thomas à Kempis.

Maxims and ethical principles by themselves are cold and lifeless. They were the lumber of the world when Christ was born into it. But when translated, incarnated into life, principles and precepts become luminous and powerful. Christ not only talked about the way and the truth and the life; He *was* the way and the truth and the life. Greatness is imitable and communicable. Man is a natural imitator. Unfortunately, in our present state, it is easier to imitate that which is evil than that which is good. The prophet said, "All we like sheep have gone astray"; and that is the way sheep go astray, by following one another. Every one of us in this respect is an example, a pattern, and an oracle to someone else.

Jesus lived a brief life upon earth, the known part of it just three years. That life was lived in a little obscure land along the Syrian coast, and His followers and associates were humble and unlearned men. And yet in that life of Jesus we find an example and a model which fits every circumstance and every condition of life, the life of those who lived under the government of Augustus and Tiberius Caesar, and the life of those who live today in London or Pittsburgh or Manila.

In all that He did, in all that He said, Christ is our example. But the one occasion in which He said definitely that He is our example, was when He was speaking on the subject of humility, His favorite virtue. At the Last Supper there had been some dispute, even on this last and saddest of nights, over who should be greatest. To impress upon them the true idea of greatness, Jesus, when supper was ended, took a towel and girded Himself and went around the table washing the feet of His disciples. When He had finished this lowly task, the task of a household servant, and had resumed His seat at the table, this is what Jesus said: "Ye call me Master and Lord: and ye say well; for so I am. If I then, your Lord and Master, have washed your feet; ye also ought to wash one another's feet. For I have given you an example, that ye should do as I have done to you. . . . If ye know these things, happy are ye if ye do them" (John 13:13-17).

Jesus well knew that it is the lack of humility, the exaltation of self, that so often leads to strife and bitterness and unhappiness in the relationship of man with man. Peter must have had that beautiful scene at the last Supper in mind, how in spite of his protests Jesus washed his feet, when he said in his letter to the disciples, "Be clothed with humility."

There was once a saint on the earth, who, wherever he went, diffused goodness as a flower does the sweetness of its odor. The angels, who had heard of this man and his influence, came down to investigate the secret of his power. So impressed were they that they summoned him to them so that they could reward him. First of all, they offered him the gift of miracles, so that by the touch of his hand he could heal the sick or raise the dead. But the saint declined the gift, saying that God alone could heal the sick. Then they offered him the power to become a model of goodness, so that men would be drawn to him by the virtue of his life. But this too the saint declined, saying that if men were drawn to him, they might be estranged from God. Then they offered him the power to convert sinners and turn men to repentance. But again the saint declined their gift, saying that only the Holy Spirit could bring men to repentance. Perplexed, the angels then asked him what he himself desired. Whereupon the saint replied: "That I might have his grace so that I might do good to men without knowing it." Thereupon the angels decreed that wherever the shadow of this saint fell, and where he himself could not see it, his shadow should cure disease and heal broken hearts and wipe away all tears. What a beautiful tribute to the power of humility!

Time would fail us to tell of some of those other riches of Christ as an example—how He is an example to us in His sympathy and pity; in His steadfast courage, that moral courage that smote to the ground the armed band that had come to take Him in Gethsemane's solitude; in His patience, purity, and sincerity. We pass over all these examples of Christ and come to the riches of His example in forgiveness of injuries. How sublime that example was! Peter must have been thinking how he cursed his Lord on that last night and denied Him, and how Jesus gave him that wonderful look that made him go out into the night and weep the sanctifying tears of repentance, when he wrote that passage about the example of Jesus: "Leaving us an example, that ye should follow his steps; who did no sin, neither was guile found in his mouth; who, when he was reviled, reviled not again" (1 Pet. 2:21). Many besides Peter reviled Jesus that night, and the next day too; but Jesus "reviled not again." Instead of reviling, he prayed for those who tortured him and mocked him at the cross, "Father, forgive them; for they know not what they do."

Between Harrisburg and Philadelphia, in an area of beautiful farming country, there lies a village embosomed in the fields, called by the pleasant scriptural name of Ephratah. In that village there once preached a humble Baptist minister. In the town was a very wicked man, who did great injury to this preacher. The War of the Revolution came on, and this wicked man joined the army of Washington. For misconduct he was court-martialed and sentenced to death. The army was then in the neighborhood of Philadelphia.

The news of the man's conviction and approaching death reached the preacher at Ephratah. Immediately he set out for Philadelphia, traveling the whole distance, more than seventy miles, on foot, and sought an audience with the commander of the army, with whom he made a plea for the life of the convicted soldier. Washington heard him through, and then said, "I am sorry, I can do nothing for your friend."

"Friend?" said the preacher. "He is the worst enemy I have in the world!"

"What!" exclaimed Washington. "And you have walked from Ephratah to Philadelphia to plead for the life of your worst enemy? That puts a new light on the case. The prisoner shall not be shot."

Here was a humble servant of Christ who had not forgotten the teachings of Jesus.

Fallen man's tribute to the example of Christ in forgiveness is revealed in the fact that when a man talks about another man having or not having the Christian spirit, what he means is the spirit of forgiveness. How many clouds are scattered, how many burdens are lifted, how many thorns are plucked, when men follow Christ's example and forgive one another. How true is that sentence with which the famous book *The Imitation of Christ* commences, "He that followeth me, walketh not in darkness."

THE RICHES OF CHRIST AS A FRIEND

It has sometimes been asserted that in contrast with pagan literature, where we find so many essays on the subject, and in contrast even with the Old Testament, where there are immortal maxims about friendship, the New Testament has very little to say on that subject. The explanation, no doubt, is that the authors of the New Testament are engrossed with the supreme friendship, the friendship of Christ. They had no time or desire to turn aside to mere human relationships and friendships because of their wonder over the friendship of Christ.

Man was made for friendship. At the beginning it was written, when man was given his best friend, a wife, "It is not good that the man should be alone." And since man was made in the image of God, God Himself seeks friends. Christ delights in friendship and in the tokens of affections. There were many who were to write of Him and speak for Him and fight for Him and die for Him; but the one person, and the only one, for whom Christ promised an immortality of fame was a woman who showed Him a beautiful token of affection when she anointed His head and His feet with the precious ointment and wiped His feet with the hair of her head. Of her He said, "wheresoever this gospel shall be preached . . . there shall also this, that this woman hath done, be told for a memorial of her" (Matt. 26:13).

Christ is the friend who does us good and not evil. It is sad but true, due to the fallen state of human nature, that the instinct and the power of friendship can be employed for evil ends. There are friends who harm instead of help. They are like the ivy which stains and decays the wall which it embraces. Samson had the wrong kind of a friend, and the wreck and ruin of his life was the consequence. Herod Antipas was stirred by the preaching of John and had noble aspirations awakened within his soul; but unfortunately he had the wrong kind of friends, and "for their sakes," and for "her sake," the sake of Herodias, he had John beheaded.

Writing to a friend, Mirabeau said of Talleyrand: "I am hoping this man is not known to you. Through the history of my misfortunes I was thrown into his hands." There are thousands of people who are in their graves, at least so far as the nobler and better part of them is concerned, whose epitaph might well be, "He had a friend." There are thousands going with heavy hearts through the labor of life who look back with sorrow and pain and poignant regret to the hour and place where they met a friend, and say of that hour and of that friend, "If I had never met him! If I had never known him!" But here is the friend who will do you good and not evil all the days of your life. Christ is the friend who not only does us good, but who awakens the good that is within our souls."

A faithful friend is also a friend who can show us our faults. Perhaps only a friend can do that. "Faithful are the wounds of a friend." One friend will let another friend go down, drift off into evil, and, however much he may regret it and lament it, he will do nothing or say nothing to stop it. "That," he says, "is his affair, not mine." But not so Jesus. He warns His friends. He warned Peter on that last night, about to be tempted, when He said to him, "Simon, Satan hath desired to have you, that he may sift you as wheat: but I have prayed for thee, that thy faith fail not" (Luke 22:31). And when Peter had been tempted and had fallen, and had cursed and denied his God, and gone out into the night to weep bitterly, he remembered that faithful friend, who was praying for him. "I have prayed for thee, that thy faith fail not." How unsearchable are the riches of a friendship like that! What a friend we have in Jesus!

THE UNSEARCHABLE RICHES OF CHRIST AS A REDEEMER

The greatest thing that one friend can do for another is to give his life for him. "Greater love hath no man than this, that a man lay down his life for his friends" (John 15:13). We have spoken of the riches of Christ as an *example* and of the riches of Christ as a *friend*. None knew better than Paul the power of Christ as an example, and he followed that example so faithfully that we are not disposed to find fault with Paul at all when he said, "Be ye followers of me, even as I also am of Christ" (1 Cor. 4:16).

None knew better than Paul the riches of Christ as a friend. Through his extraordinary life he put that friendship to the utmost test, and so far as history and experience are concerned, Paul, even above John, deserves the title "that disciple whom Jesus loved." Paul's last comment on that friendship was just when the darkness of death was coming down over him, when he said that all men had forsaken him, but "the Lord stood with me, and strengthened me. . . . And the Lord shall deliver me from every evil work, and will preserve me unto his heavenly kingdom: to whom be glory forever and ever. Amen" (2 Tim. 4:17). Paul's past experience with the friendship of Jesus had been such that no shadow of doubt as to that friendship falls across the path of the future.

But when he speaks here about the unsearchable riches of Christ, what is uppermost in his mind is the unsearchable riches of Christ as a *redeemer*. That was the inexhaustible, the unsearchable, the inexpressible riches of Christ. Christ is inexhaustible in the riches of His person as a redeemer. The infinite God, and yet the perfect man, who knows our sorrows and our temptations. He is inexhaustible in the riches of His love as a redeemer. Love is the greatest thing in man. It is also the greatest thing in God, "God *so* loved the world." What is meant by that "so"? What is meant is the measureless extent of that redeeming love of God in Christ. I have sometimes thought that the most beautiful love in the world is love of a mother for a crippled or deformed or mentally deficient child; and other times I have thought that the most wonderful love on earth is the love of a mother for a son who is a criminal in the penitentiary. But beautiful though that love is, what is it compared with the marvelous love of Christ for you and me as sinners? "While we were yet sinners, Christ died for us" (Rom. 5:8).

Unsearchable too are the riches of Christ's pardon for sin, that wonderful device whereby mercy and truth kiss one another, whereby the holiness and justice of God are upheld and vindicated and satisfied, and sin is punished, and yet the sinner is pardoned and forgiven and justified. No wonder the angels want to look into the riches of that! No wonder when Paul thought of it he cried out, "The unsearchable riches of Christ!" And again: "O the depth of the riches both of the wisdom and knowledge of God! How unsearchable are his judgments, and his way past finding out!" (Rom. 11:33).

Unsearchable too are the riches of the joy of that redemption in the life to come. Who can explore that? Who can measure "the powers of the world to come," the final blessing and enduement and glory of the divine redemption? The best we can do is to do what Paul said, when he threw up his hands and cried out: "Eye hath not seen, nor ear heard, neither have entered into the heart of man, the things which God hath prepared for them that love him" (1 Cor. 2:9).

"Unto you therefore which believe," said Peter, "he is precious" (1 Pet. 2:7). Only those who believe can know the riches of Christ as a redeemer. You may know Him as a teacher, as an example, but do you know Him as a redeemer? Do you know Him as the One who has led you to the foot of the cross, the friend of sinners, who loved you and gave Himself for you?

11

THE MYSTERY OF GODLINESS

And without controversy great is the mystery of godliness: God was manifest
in the flesh, justified in the spirit, seen of angels, preached among the nations,
believed on in the world, received up into glory (1 Timothy 3:16).

Sunset over the Ephesian plains. The yellow fields and hills are
turning amber. On the top of the highest hill we can see the
circular seats of the amphitheater. On the other side of the city
stand the immense columns of the Temple of Diana, and in the
distance the westering sun turns the Aegean into a sea of glass
mingled with fire. The south wind is blowing in softly from the
sea. Walking along the famous Corso, the marble avenue lined
with the busts of the emperors and the images of the gods, and
crowded with throngs of people, some of them going to the Temple
of Diana, but most of them to the bloody shows of the
amphitheater, we make our way into a humbler part of the city,
where there is another temple, a temple which cannot vie in
splendor with the great Temple of Diana, but the worship of
which and the faith of which will before long empty the Temple
of Diana and all the temples of pagan worship.

Passing through this humble part of the city, we pause before an open door as we catch the sound of singing. Listen to
that song! The voices of old men and women, matron and
maid, young man and little children, are lifting that song. Listen! This is what we hear: "God was manifest in the flesh,
justified in the spirit, seen of angels, preached among the na-

tions, believed on in the world, received up into glory" (1 Tim. 3:16).

In a memorable letter Pliny the Younger, governor of Bithynia, a province on the Black Sea, wrote to the Emperor Trajan asking how he should proceed against the Christians, whose worship was already outlawed, and whose beliefs he stigmatized as "an odious superstition." He told the emperor that the Christians were accustomed to meet together on the morning of a fixed day, evidently Sunday, when they took vows not to rob or steal or lie or commit adultery, and that they sang "a hymn of praise to Christ as God." It is just possible that this passage, which is in rhythmic and poetic form, was one of those hymns of praise to Christ as God which Pliny's spies heard the Christians of Bithynia sing. But whether part of an old hymn quoted by Paul or—what is more likely—the words of the apostle himself in a moment of high inspiration, this passage is one of the most sublime in the Bible, and also one of the noblest summaries of our Christian faith.

Paul was a man who could rise easily from the ordinary and commonplace to the sublime. He has been telling Timothy, in charge of the church at Ephesus, about the proper conduct of ministers and worshipers, and how they ought to behave themselves in the house of God. From that disciplinary subject he rises in a moment to this grand delineation of the Christian faith: "The house of God, which is . . . the pillar and ground of the truth" (1 Tim. 3:15). This was a metaphor borrowed from the greatest temple of antiquity, the Temple of Diana, with its beautiful jasper columns. All that remains of it today are a few drums of its pillars lying in the midst of a great desolation. But how magnificent that temple was, one can judge by the columns which uphold the dome of St. Sophia in Constantinople, columns which the Emperor Justinian the Great took from the ruins of the Temple of Diana to use in building his great church in the sixth century.

The pillars of that temple were in keeping with the majesty of the temple itself. When Paul, then, says that the church of God is the pillar and ground of the truth, what he means is that, as the pillar upholds the temple and is in keeping with its greatness, so the church upholds the gospel, the revealed truth of Christianity. "Great," declares Paul, "is the mystery of godliness." By that he did not mean what mystery means to you and me today, something which is inexplicable and inscrutable. "Mystery" is Paul's favorite word for Christianity, and by mystery he means the great secret of man's redemption and salvation, hid from time eternal, but now revealed in Christ and proclaimed by His church. How great that mystery—that gospel—is, he declares in successive phrases, each one of which is like the pulsation of a mighty chord of music.

"GOD WAS MANIFEST IN THE FLESH"

You could not say of even the greatest and most renowned of men that they were God manifest in the flesh. It would be absurd to speak of them so, for their life history began at their birth. But not so with Christ. He was God manifest in the flesh. "The Word was made flesh, and dwelt among us." That was John's way of putting it. Paul puts it thus: "Great is the mystery of godliness: God was manifest in the flesh."

All true Christianity depends upon that fact. Upon that rests Christ's authority as an example. Christ, you say, is the supreme example. But how do you know that He is? You say that He is the supreme teacher. But how do you know that? You believe in Christ as your Savior and your Redeemer. "But," one asks, "how do you know that He is the only Savior and Redeemer? There are those today who follow other examples and other teachers and other saviors." The only reason for our belief that Christ is our supreme example, our supreme teacher, and our only Savior, is that He who walked the dusty Syrian roads and stooped to touch with the hand of pity the leper, the palsied, and the blind, who spake the parables, was forsaken, denied, betrayed, sold for thirty pieces of silver, mocked and scourged and spat upon, crowned with thorns and crucified upon a cross, was "God over all," "manifest in the flesh." Save as I would take an interest in the moving story of the death of any great man—of Moses or Socrates or Stephen, the first martyr, or John Huss— I have no deep interest in what occurred on that cross, on that skull-shaped hill at Jerusalem nearly twenty centuries ago, unless the One who suffered and died there was in truth God manifest in the flesh.

The manner in which Christ was manifest in the flesh—that is, the Virgin Birth, as related in Matthew and Luke, about which there has been, and strangely, so much discussion and debate and unbelief—was in beautiful harmony with the nature of the Person who came into the world and the purpose of His coming, which was to redeem the world. If God was to be manifest in the flesh, in what other way ought He to have come? That He came in the sublime manner related in the Gospels leaves the truth of His coming, the mode of His manifestation in the flesh, as clear as the stars, as fair as the angels, and as tender as a mother's love.

"JUSTIFIED IN THE SPIRIT"

Jesus was made manifest in the flesh, that is, in a human nature just like our own. But, in contrast with you and me, He was justified in His spirit. You and I, as sinners and unjust, are justified by faith in the redeeming work of Christ on the cross. But Christ Himself needed no such sacrifice of justification, for He was justified in His spirit—that is, He was blameless and sinless in His own life.

This is a miracle that the world has seen only once, and will never see again. "Which of you," Christ asks, "convinceth me of sin?" (John 8:46). Satan came to tempt Him and, if possible, to discredit Him and condemn Him, but Jesus said that he "hath nothing in me." Even the most saintly persons, those who appear to us most free from the taint of sin, lament their shortcomings and transgressions and confess that they must put their hope and trust in the redeeming work of Christ. But Christ needed no redeemer. He was a man of like passions with us. He knew hunger, thirst, sorrow, pain, loneliness, and temptation, for He was tempted in all points like as we are. But in the moral realm, in the realm of right and wrong, Christ is altogether apart, supreme and unique. Alone of all men since the Fall, He knew the joy of a conscience void of offense. It is always a mistake—and bordering on irreverence—to speak, as some do, of Jesus as the first or greatest or only Christian. Jesus was not a Christian. A Christian is a sinner who puts his trust in Christ for salvation. But Christ Himself needed no savior.

The least shadow upon the character and person of Christ would have disqualified Him to be our Redeemer. But where is that fault, or shadow of fault? What would you change in His history? What word did He speak that He ought not to have spoken? What word did He leave unsaid that He ought to have said? What prayer did He breathe that He ought not to have prayed? What did He leave undone that He ought to have done? What look or attitude or sigh or cry, what permission or what refusal, is there that you would have blotted out of the record? No, there is not one. He was "justified in the spirit." Christ has stood the hardest of all tests, the test of life and the test of time. The New England dreamer and seer, Bronson Alcott, on a visit to England, had a conversation with Carlyle in which he said that he could sincerely say, just as much as Jesus, that he was "one with the Father." "Yes," replied Carlyle, "but Jesus got men to believe him!" Only a sinless Christ, one who was justified in His spirit, could have led men to believe in Him.

"SEEN OF ANGELS"

Now we behold the grand sweep of Paul's inspired imagination. He likes to relate the redeeming work of Christ to the whole universe. That work was done, so far as we know, for the salvation of men on this planet, and for no others. But it was done also in the presence of and with the admiration and wonder of, the whole company of heavenly and unfallen beings. Man has no monopoly on created intelligence. In *Paradise Lost* Milton says:

> Nor think, though men were none,
> That heaven would want spectators, God want praise.
> Millions of spiritual creatures walk the earth
> Unseen, both when we wake, and when we sleep:
> All these with ceaseless praise his works behold
> Both day and night.

The whole population of the heavenly worlds was interested in the mission of Christ. Angels foretold the birth of Christ, sang over Bethlehem when He was born, strengthened Him in His temptation, comforted Him in Gethsemane, sat by His empty tomb, were the first preachers of His resurrection, comforted His disciples at His ascension, and declared that Christ would come again in the clouds with the angels in great glory.

There are several passages in the New Testament which would indicate that the tragedy of human history, and the tragedy of Calvary, was enacted not only for the benefit of mankind, and for the redemption of man, but for the instruction and inspiration of the angels and the unfallen spirits. Paul declared, "We are made a spectacle unto the world, and to angels and to men" (1 Cor. 4:9). And again, he said that the coming of Christ and His atonement was "to the intent that now unto the principalities and powers in heavenly places might be known by the church the manifold wisdom of God" (Eph. 3:10). And again, Peter declared that the angels desire to look into the work of Christ as a redeemer: "Which things the angels desire to look into" (1 Pet. 1:12).

> Angels in fixed amazement,
>   Around our altars hover;
> With eager gaze adore the grace
>   Of our eternal Lover.

"Preached Among the Nations, Believed on in the World"

Christ is the only truth worth preaching to the nations. Ever since He told His disciples to go into all the world and preach the gospel to every creature, the story of divine love has been told. John saw an angel "fly in the midst of heaven, having the everlasting gospel to preach" (Rev. 14:6). Still that angel flies in the midst of heaven. Still Christ is preached among the nations and believed on in the world.

"Believed on in the world." There is a phrase which ought to make every chord of our souls vibrate with joy and wonder. When Jesus rose from the dead, some doubted, but some believed. When Paul preached Christ and the Resurrection on Mars' Hill, the philosophers laughed at him; but "certain men clave unto him, and believed, among the which was Dionysius the Areopagite, and a woman named Damaris" (Acts 17:34). Yes, wherever Christ has been uplifted and preached there have been those who "clave unto him."

"Believed on in the world." Yes, and in *this* world, a world so clouded with darkness, so rebellious against God and the truth, so haunted with devils, so cruel and dark and cynical a world. In such a world as *this*, men have believed on Christ. Always there have been those who were ready to say: "Who shall separate us from the love of Christ? Shall tribulation, or distress, or persecution, or famine, or nakedness, or peril, or sword? . . . Nay, in all these things we are more than conquerors through him that loved us. For I am persuaded, that neither death, nor life, nor angels, nor principalities, nor powers, nor things present, nor things to come, nor height, nor depth, nor any other creature, shall be able to separate us from the love of God, which is in Christ Jesus our Lord" (Rom. 8:35-39).

"Received Up into Glory"

The finished work of Christ and also the prophecy of the final victory is declared in the phrase "received up into glory." What a day it must have been when Christ ascended into heaven, having "led captivity captive," perhaps releasing from the bonds of death and taking into the glory of heaven with him the souls of the righteous dead—Abraham, Moses, Elijah, Isaiah, David, and the first fruits of His cross, that penitent thief, to whom He said, "today shalt thou be with me in paradise" (Luke 23:43). Oh, if the angels sang in wonder when Christ came down to earth and was manifest in the flesh, how they must have sung when He came back to heaven, having led captivity captive! What a song that must have been! What a shout must have gone up when the angels called on the twelve gates of heaven to lift up their everlasting doors and let the King of Glory in!

I am sure that all the angels were there to greet Him, from the angels who swung their swords at the gates of the lost Eden to the angel of the Apocalypse, who stood with one foot upon the land and one foot upon the sea, and sware by Him who lives forever and ever that time should be no more. Raphael, the Angel of Reason, was there to bow before the sublime reason of the cross. Uriel, the Angel of Light, was there to quench his light before the Light of the world. Michael, the Angel of the Sword, was there to sheathe his sword in the presence of Him who brings peace to the earth. And Gabriel, the Angel of Song, was there to rejoice in the finished work of Christ, and to lead all the choirs of heaven as they sang not in prophecy only, but in glorious consummation, "Glory to God in the highest, and on earth peace, good will toward men" (Luke 2:14).

This, then, is the "mystery of godliness." This is the faith which established the church of the living God in the world, so that the gates of hell have not prevailed against it. But the world is still evil; it still casts up its mire and dirt. It is a world still bleeding from its ghastly, self-inflicted wounds, a world still alienated from God. The need of the world is the same today as when Christ was first manifest in the flesh. And thank God He is the same Christ, the same yesterday, today, and forever.

This Christ of the ages is for you and for me. With all His pre-existent glory, His oneness with the Father, His adoration by the angels and the hosts of heaven, He is also the Christ for you and for me—for our every need, our every problem, our every sorrow, our every sin. If you know Him and love Him now, cleave to Him unto the end! If you have not chosen Him, then I call upon you to do so: "Choose you this day whom ye will serve." Why serve others, as other men do? Why not serve the everlasting Christ, and join the ranks that grow in number from age to age, the ranks of those who have believed on Him in this world, and who, as the ransomed of the Lord, shall one day return and come to Zion with songs and everlasting joy upon their heads?

12

THE SIN WHICH DOTH BESET US

Let us lay aside every weight, and the sin which doth so easily beset us,
and let us run with patience the race that is set before us (Hebrews 12:1).

The sea is like sapphire, the sky cloudless and of the deepest
blue. The air is soft and the sunshine warm. In the distance
are the graceful brown columns of a Greek temple. Along the
highway running from the temple to the stadium are busts and
tablets where are inscribed the names of the winners in the
Olympian and Isthmian games in past years. Along the race course
rise, tier upon tier, the marble seats of the stadium, crowded today
with visitors from all parts of the Greek world who have come for
the annual celebration of the games.

Presently there is the sharp, clear, commanding note of the
herald's trumpet. A hush comes over the expectant throng. From
out of their training booths come the racers, trained to the moment, not an ounce of superfluous flesh sagging from their
splendidly molded bodies, bronzed by the Peloponesian sunlight.
At another blast from the trumpet they take their place on the
starting line, every muscle tense and set. Among the thousands
who line the course not a word, not even a whisper, is heard.
Suddenly there rings out the third blast on the trumpet, and the
racers are off like an arrow, straining for the distant goal. Save for
a loincloth, they are naked. For months they have trained for this
race, abstaining from strong drink and rich foods and the pleasures of the world. The ambition of each racer's life is to have his

name inscribed on one of those memorial tablets and to have the laurel crown of victory placed upon his brow. As they flash down the course, their friends on the marble seats, who happen to be from that part of Greece from which a particular runner comes, shout their encouragement to them.

That is the picture the writer had in mind when he wrote this famous and familiar verse: "Let us lay aside every weight, and the sin which doth so easily beset us, and let us run with patience the race that is set before us." Like that race in the Corinthian or Olympian games, the Christian life is a race which calls for self-denial, concentration, ambition, and endurance unto the end. The Olympian runners were striving for a corruptible crown, a crown of leaves. The Christian runner is striving for an incorruptible crown, the crown of glory. Yet how many there are engaged in this Christian race who give little impression of its seriousness and of the prize which is at stake. Some of them are slumped down in slumber; others have paused to take refreshment by the way; others are leaning over the barrier, holding converse with their friends on the benches; others are carrying over their shoulders costly and heavy garments; others are hobbled with some evil habit, and others are caught and enmeshed in sin. And yet this is the real race. If we are going to win the crown, we must, as those ancient runners did, "lay aside every weight, and the sin which doth so easily beset us."

Sin is not a popular subject, but it is still a popular fact. Sin is no longer a popular subject, even in the pulpit. An examination of forty-four sermons preached sometime ago in metropolitan pulpits disclosed that there was only *one* mention of sin. But sin is still a popular fact. It is the source of all the woe and sorrow of mankind. Its shadow is as universal as human nature and as eternal as human history.

The older preachers used to speak of "original sin." This is rarely mentioned now. But, like many of those now-abandoned theological terms, "it stands for a great reality—that human nature is fallen, and that the weeds of evil grow easily and quickly in the soil of human lives." Suppose you were to take two of the most high-minded and best-instructed persons in the world today, heirs to the best in our culture, civilization, education, and, I may say, Christianity, and cut them off entirely from the influences of our world. Suppose you were to settle them upon some island, separated from all the rest of mankind. Still, in another 6,000 years the race descended from them would manifest the same traits and show the same kind of civilization that we behold today. And why is this? Because human nature has not changed from age to age, and in every age and under every condition man's natural tendency is downward.

In addition to this, the natural inclination of man's heart, there is the state of the world outside of man, where are continual incitements to evil. And always, back of all else, is man's eternal foe, the Prince of Evil, Satan himself, who seeks to ruin the souls of men. But beyond all this, or with all this, is the fact that there are peculiar and particular and besetting sins. Always in men there is a difference in individuality and character. They come into the world with particular traits and tendencies.

There are those who have a tendency in the direction of good, for almost every life has some efflorescence of that which is good. But there are also tendencies in the other direction. It is in this evil inclination that sin discovers its affinity and does its fatal injury.

Moses was a magnificent man, but he had a tendency to impatience and anger. Saul was a magnificent man, but his life was poisoned by jealousy. David was a magnificent man, but his life was corrupted by sensuality. Peter was a magnificent man, but he had a weakness on the side of cowardice. When the writer to the Hebrews says, "Let us lay aside every weight, and the sin which doth so easily beset us," he exempts none from this duty and necessity, for all have them.

A man once had a dream that he stood at the foot of a wide, dazzling, marble stairway leading up to the entrance to heaven, and the height of it was so great that the top was lost to view. On the lowest step he saw a box of chalk and inscribed thereon these words: "Each aspirant, on his ascent to the mansions above, must take a piece of chalk and write a sin committed in the previous world on each step before mounting it." In obedience to these directions, the man took a piece of chalk and started up the stairway, writing some remembered sin on each step as he advanced. When he had gone some distance, he stood still, unable to remember any more. But suddenly, as he looked up, he saw a dark, rugged figure hurriedly descending. As it drew near he recognized it to be none other than the archbishop of Canterbury. The man exclaimed, "Your Grace, who would have expected to see you here? Have they refused you admission?" Whereupon a gruff, harsh voice ejaculated: "No, but I've used up all my chalk! Coming down for more!" That dream embodied truth.

It is always easier, of course, to note a besetting sin in the life of someone else than it is to note our own besetting sin. But it is there. With one it may be discontent, an unthankful heart; with another, envy; with another, jealousy; with another, harsh and severe judgment; with another, oversensitiveness, always imagining evil thought or done against one; with another, cynicism; with another, sloth, laziness; with another, cowardice; with another dishonesty; with another, the sins of the tongue; and with another, an evil appetite or the sins of the flesh. But whatever it is, it must be laid aside. The soul and that sin cannot win the race together.

A besetting sin is often the source and parent of other sins, because it is through that besetting sin that evil has its grip upon our hearts. If you have ever tried to dig up a bush or a small tree, you have discovered that there is one particular tap root which anchors the tree in the earth. You may cut all the other roots, but until you cut that one root, you cannot get the tree out. But if you cut that one root, it is easy to cut the others and remove the tree. So does the besetting sin hold a man to this world.

One besetting sin has great and dangerous power to hinder us and retard us in our Christian life. In 31 B.C was fought the great battle of Actium, off the west coast of Greece, where the fleet of Octavius defeated the squadrons of Mark Antony and Cleopatra. There was a tradition that in the midst of the battle Mark Antony's warship unaccountably slackened its speed, and then, in spite of the united efforts of hundreds of slaves toiling at the oars, and a strong wind filling the sails, came to a standstill. A diver was sent down to examine the hull of the ship and brought up a little fish which, according to the superstition of that day, could, by attaching itself to the hull of a vessel, hold the largest ship motionless in the water. Even a noted scientist like Pliny the Elder, commenting on that supposition, said; "What is more violent than the sea and the wind? What greater work of art than a ship? Yet one little fish can hold back all their fury. The winds may blow, the waves may rage, but this small creature controls their fury and stops a vessel when chains and anchor would not hold her, and that it does, not by hard labor, but merely by adhering to her."

To us that is an idle tale, a foolish superstition. But when we transfer it to the moral history of man, it is no fable, but a true parable of life. A single besetting sin, adhering to a man's life, can bring his spiritual progress to a standstill. In vain are the winds of better aspiration, in vain the exhortations of others, in vain the pull on the oars of his resolution and prayers. One sin has brought the ship of his soul to a standstill.

A besetting sin, even one unnoted by ourselves, will check and retard the spiritual life. The first time I saw the ocean, although I had once crossed the ocean without remembering it, was at San Pedro. When I saw the great ocean, I felt as Balboa did when he looked on the vast Pacific. And here at San Pedro were the ships with their tall masts, for sailing ships were then still plentiful. What a thrill it was to look upon them as they lay at anchor in the harbor!

With my brother I got into a rowboat and started to row across the harbor to Dead Man's Island, now vanished, but once a well-known landmark and familiar to all readers of *Two Years Before the Mast*. Halfway around to the island, our boat seemed to move very slowly, and it took the combined push of four oars to move it at all. Finally we looked over the edge toward the keel of the boat and saw that a small strip of iron had become bent and protruded down into the sea, and that a mass of seaweed had accumulated about it. That was why it was difficult for us to move the boat. So about a single besetting sin there may gather a mass of objects and hindrances which will stop completely the onward progress of the soul.

Because of the dragging back and dragging down power of one besetting sin in a man's life, we see what the apostle means when he says that in this race for eternal life we must lay aside every sin.

In one of the famous battles of the Old Testament, the king of Judah, Jehoshaphat, and the king of Israel, Ahab, went up to fight against the fortress of Ramoth-gilead, in the possession of the Syrian army under the command of Benhadad. Before the battle was joined, the king of Syria called together his thirty-two Captains and gave them these instructions: "Fight neither with small nor great, save only with the king of Israel" (1 Kings 22:31). They knew that when Ahab was killed or driven from the field the victory would be won, for he was the heart and center of the confederacy against Syria.

Knowing that he would be the object of special attack, Ahab had disguised himself in the garb of a common soldier. But he could not avoid the shaft of judgment and retribution. "A certain man drew a bow at a venture, and smote the king of Israel between the joints of the harness" (1 Kings 22:34). Mortally stricken, Ahab turned his chariot out of the battle and died at the going down of the sun. His death was soon followed by the defeat and rout of his army. The fallen king meant a fallen cause.

And there is a parable for the welfare of life! Make war on the besetting sin! Fight neither with small nor with great, save against it; and when you do that, you make war against all the evil that is in your life. When that besetting sin is conquered, then you are on the road to victory.

How splendidly Paul—I am one of those who think that Paul is the author of this letter to the Hebrews—how splendidly he lifts this theme of fighting against ordinary commonplace, ugly, and dangerous sins to the highest! What he says here comes at the close of one of the sublimest portions of the Bible. It is unfortunate that there is a break in the very midst of the apostle's grand climax, and that the great passage is broken into two chapters. The twelfth chapter starts with this verse: "Wherefore seeing we also are compassed about with so great a cloud of witnesses, let us lay aside every weight, and the sin which doth so easily beset us, and let us run with patience the race that is set before us." But that conclusion follows the great chapter in which he has called the roll of the heroes of faith, those who, through faith, overcame— from Abel and Enoch and Noah and Abraham and Moses, down to Samuel and the prophets. "Wherefore," Paul says, "seeing we also are compassed about with so great a cloud of witnesses."

Perhaps one cannot say that the writer states here as a fact that the noble and illustrious dead actually hold us in survey and observe us as we fight our battle, for the word "witness" here may be used in the sense of one who has stood for the truth of God, and from that comes our word "martyr," one who witnesses for God. The glorious company of all those who have lived and died for the faith proclaim to us the greatness of our warfare, and how in Christ we can come off conquerors and more than conquerors.

But if the writer does not definitely say that the glorious dead actually behold us and watch us now in our present warfare, and as we run our race, he certainly does *not* say that they do not or cannot. A fair inference would be that just as the spectators on the crowded benches of the amphitheaters and stadia watched and cheered on their friends who ran in the races, so the noble dead behold you and me. It is in the presence of all history and of all heaven that you live your life and fight your battle as a Christian.

How inspiring it is to think of that! Not only have I before me the example of the noble and illustrious heroes of faith, but perhaps it is granted to them actually to behold me in my race. Yonder they are! Yonder is the gallery of the patriarchs, Abraham and Isaac and Jacob; and yonder the gallery of the prophets, Moses and Elijah and Samuel and Jeremiah. And yonder is the gallery of the apostles, Peter and John and Paul. And yonder is the gallery of the martyrs, all those who died for truth, Abel and Isaiah and Stephen and Justin Martyr and Polycarp, all those who "loved not their lives unto the death." And yonder is the gallery of the reformers, Josiah and Nehemiah and Luther and Calvin and Knox. And yonder is the gallery of the great preachers, Chrysostom and Peter and Jonah and Chalmers and Beecher and Spurgeon. And yonder is the gallery of the great missionaries, Augustine and Patrick and Livingstone and Moffatt and Paton. And yonder is the gallery of the great singers, David and Bernard of Clairvaux and Isaac Watts and Toplady and Charles Wesley.

But there is yet another gallery which means far more to you perhaps than the gallery of the martyrs or the prophets or the apostles or the patriarchs. It is the gallery where sit your own mother, father, husband, wife, brother, sister, whose warfare is accomplished, and who now, clad in white, follow the Lamb. They are the witnesses who compass you about and inspire you to fidelity, who behold your conflict and rejoice in your victory. And about them all, and greater than them all, the greatest warrior of them all, the greatest conqueror of them all, is our Lord and Savior, Jesus Christ, the Author, the Captain, and the Finisher of our faith. When you look to him you cannot fail. And with all those who in past ages have overcome through faith, one day you will stand acknowledged, victorious, and sinless, by the side of your divine Redeemer and sing His power to save.

13

THE SAME YESTERDAY, TODAY, FOREVER

Jesus Christ the same yesterday, and today, and forever   (Hebrews 13:8).

It was seven twenty-two on the morning of April 15, 1865. The gaunt form stretched on the bed in the room in the house on Tenth Street ceased to breathe. The Secretary of War, Edwin M. Stanton, turned to the window and pulled down the blind to shut out the bright sunlight. Then, turning again and looking down at the silent form, he said, "Now he belongs to the ages."

That is the shortest biography of Lincoln—and one of the best. Yet, after all, there is only one who "belongs to the ages." It is He to whom the ages belong, Jesus Christ, "the same yesterday, and today, and forever."

There are some texts which haunt the preacher and yet frighten him. They are too great to preach on, and yet too great to omit. Here is one of them. When you pronounce it, you strike a sublime chord which echoes all the music of divine creation, revelation, redemption, the morning stars singing together, the patriarchs, the goodly fellowship of the prophets, the noble army of the martyrs, the glorious company of the apostles, and the music of that last day when the kingdoms of this world shall have become the kingdoms of our Lord, and of His Christ.

High up on the mountainside, overlooking the ancient city of Antioch, is a cavern where, according to tradition, the early Christian disciples used to meet, and where Peter preached to them. Standing in front of that cavern one looks down upon the city with its mosques and minarets, its markets and bazaars, the great water wheels going slowly around, the gigantic plane trees, with their branches bending before the afternoon breeze, and the Orontes River, cold and gray from the snow of the mountains, flowing rapidly through the city and under the bridges. That river has been ever changing from hour to hour, from day to day, from year to year, and from age to age, like the humanity which has crossed those bridges from the days of Chrysostom down to the present hour. But the mountain which looks down upon it is just the same as when Peter and the first disciples in Antioch met there to break bread and praise the name of their Redeemer. So Christ looks down upon the ever-changing stream of human history.

> Time like an ever-rolling stream
> Bears all its sons away.

But Christ is the same, "yesterday, and today, and forever." The major theme of the book of Hebrews is the immutable Christ. The author first of all contrasts the changeless Christ with the changing universe. "They shall perish; but thou remainest; and they shall all wax old as doth a garment; and as a vesture thou shalt fold them up, and they shall be changed: but thou art the same, and thy years shall not fail" (Heb. 1:12). Then he contrasts the immutability of Christ as a redeemer, a sacrifice for sin, with the changing procession of the high priests, who once in the year, on the great Day of Atonement, went behind the veil of the temple to sprinkle the blood upon the mercy seat. But Christ is the eternal Priest, who through the eternal Spirit offered Himself on the cross, once for all, to bear the sins of many.

Then the author contrasts the changing kingdoms of this world with the changeless kingdom of Christ. These kingdoms are shaken down that the things which cannot be shaken may remain, for we receive a kingdom which cannot be moved. And finally he contrasts the changelessness of Jesus, as a friend and teacher and companion, with the ever-changing friendships and associations of this life. He calls the roll of the heroes of faith, from Abel down to David and Samuel. These all, having served their day and generation, disappeared. By this time too the Christian disciples had lost in death many of their friends and loved ones, many of those who had spoken unto them the Word of God—and not a few of them no doubt had died the martyr's death. It is in this particular connection that he flings out the grand music of the text, "Jesus Christ the same yesterday, and today, and forever."

In the days of the pioneers the frontier preachers often had to ride their horses through swollen rivers where there were no bridges or ferries. If they looked down at the turbid, raging flood about them, they were apt to become dizzy and fall from the saddle and be swept away. But if they fixed their eye upon a great oak on the further bank or a jutting rock or hilltop, they passed through in safety. Here, then is a text for troubled times, a troubled world, and for troubled souls. In the midst of the swelling flood, the ever-rolling stream of time, let us lift our eyes to the eternal Christ, immutable in His person, in His teaching, and as a redeemer.

CHRIST IS IMMUTABLE IN HIS PERSON

"The same yesterday, and today, and forever." All that He is today, He was yesterday. All that He was yesterday, He is today. All that He will be tomorrow, He is today. All that He is today, He will be forever.

"The same yesterday." How far back that takes us! Before the mountains were brought forth, or ever He had formed the earth and the world, Christ was the same. He was the same when the morning stars sang together, and all the sons of God shouted for joy. He was the same when Abraham rejoiced to see His day, and Moses wrote of Him. He was the same when Balaam, apostate but eloquent prophet, standing on the mountain peak in Moab, cried out: "I shall see him, but not now: I shall behold him, but not nigh: there shall come a Star out of Jacob, and a Scepter shall rise out of Israel" (Num. 24:17). He was the same when David sang of His everlasting kingdom. He was the same when Isaiah painted that masterpiece of His suffering and His triumph. He was the same when the star halted over Bethlehem.

He was the same when He was transfigured in glory on the mount, when He was betrayed and denied and spat upon and crowned with thorns and hung upon a cross between two thieves and murderers. He was the same when He rose again from the dead and ascended into heaven and poured out the Holy Spirit on the church. He was the same when the dying Stephen saw Him standing at the right hand of God. He was the same when Paul and John and Peter and

Chrysostom and Augustine and Calvin and Luther and Whitefield and Spurgeon and Moody declared His redeeming love. He was the same when your fathers and mothers told you of His love. He was the same when you gave your youthful heart to Christ. The same today that He was yesterday, the same yesterday that He is today.

CHRIST IS IMMUTABLE AS A TEACHER OF DIVINE TRUTH

Man's three great questions are these: What can I know? What ought I to do? For what can I hope? Christ answers all these questions. What can I know? I can know God, whom to know aright is life eternal. What ought I to do? I ought to do the will of God and follow in His steps. For what can I hope? I can hope for a happy and blessed immortality, beyond the sphere of sin and grief and death. As a teacher Christ never changes. This is in contrast with earthly teachers and earthly systems. The vaunted conceptions and convictions of the history and philosophy and science of one day may be the jest of tomorrow. But Christ never changes.

Which one of His sayings has become obsolete or outmoded, no longer applicable? Which one needs revision? "Our Father who art in heaven, hallowed be thy name"? "Forgive us our debts, as we forgive our debtors"? "Lead us not into temptation"? "Judge not, that ye be not judged"? "It is more blessed to give than to receive"? "Blessed are the pure in heart: for they shall see God"? Which one of these sayings is obsolete today?

No; Christ has stood that severest of all tests, the test of time. What He taught in the streets of Capernaum He teaches in a thousand villages today. What He taught in Jerusalem He teaches in London and New York. What He taught on the banks of the Jordan and on the shores of the Sea of Galilee He teaches on the banks of the Thames and the Hudson. As long as the heart has passions, as long as life has woes, the words of Jesus will speak to the soul of man. "Heaven and earth shall pass away, but my words shall not pass away" (Matt. 24:35).

When John saw Him in His great vision on the isle of Patmos, standing in the midst of the seven golden candlesticks, with the seven stars in His right hand, and His countenance flaming like the sun, and fell at His feet as one dead, Jesus lifted Him up and said, "Fear not; I am the first and the last: I am he that liveth, and was dead; and, behold, I am alive for evermore, Amen; and have the keys of hell and of death" (Rev. 1:18). Today a struggling, suffering mankind wants to know who has the keys. "Who will show us any good?"

Education does not have the keys. Once we thought it did. We have invested the revenues of empires in our system of education. We have put a college on every high hill, and a schoolhouse under every green tree. But notwithstanding, every year in our land millions of major crimes are committed, a major crime every few seconds. And of this great army of criminals the majority are youths in their teens. No; secular education does not have the keys.

Science does not have the keys. Once we thought it did, and the world has worshiped at its altar, beseeching it to break all chains and heal all wounds and open blind eyes. But now mankind wonders what new and terrible device the mind of man will devise and the hand of man will fabricate to rain down destruction and death and woe upon his head. Science does not have the keys.

The political leaders and statesmen do not have the keys. They are but men of like passions with you and me, and there is no reason to expect that men and nations will not again attempt the golden portals of the future with the blood-rusted key of the past.

Only Christ has the keys. Today again we hear His voice as He confronts the weary nations: "I am he that liveth, and was dead; . . . and, behold, I . . . have the keys." "I am the way."

CHRIST IS IMMUTABLE AS THE REDEEMER FROM SIN

The cross is the eternal fact looking *backward*. Christ is the Lamb of God slain from the foundation of the world. The cross is the eternal fact looking *forward;* for, whenever the pencil of the Holy Spirit pries open for a little the windows of heaven, that is the music that you hear floating down over the earth: "Unto him that loved us, and washed us from our sins in his own blood, . . . be glory and dominion forever and ever" (1 Pet. 4:11).

There are not wanting those today who, either in theory or in practice, leave out Christ as the immutable, the once-for-all Redeemer from sin. The great, the real Christ, they tell us, is the moralist, the educator, the social reformer. This other Christ, the redeeming Christ, either does not exist at all, or, if He does exist, that is the least important aspect of His work and office. But since

I have put all my hope in this redeeming Christ, since I have committed unto Him all that I have against that day, if I have been mistaken, then I want to know it, and I want to know it now. Is the real Christ the social reconstructor, the great expert on the race question? Or is He the Christ who loved me and gave Himself for me, who has written my name on the palms of His hands, who brought the doxologies rolling from the lips of the apostles and the martyrs, who emptied the blood-stained arenas and colosseums of their shouting throngs, who overturned the altars in the pagan temples, who broke the shackles of the slaves, who lifted up woman and made her man's companion, who threw a zone of mercy around the helplessness of childhood, who has inspired a never-ending hymn of praise and love from His followers, who warms the heart of those who can say of Him, "My beloved is mine, and I am his," who started the processions winding over the hills and through the valleys and across the streams on the mornings of the Lord's Day to the little white churches in the wildwood?

Who can tell me? Where shall I go? I will go first to the mighty and unfallen intelligences of heaven—to Uriel, the Angel of Light who stands in the sun; to Raphael, the Angel of Reason; to Michael, the Angel with the Sword; and to Gabriel, the Angel of Holy Song— and I will ask them: "Mighty angels, is the Christ before whose presence you veil your faces, crying, 'Holy! Holy! Holy!' the Christ in whom I put my trust?" And with all the music of heaven, with a voice like the sound of many waters, they answer, "He is the same!"

I will go to Abraham and Moses, and I will ask them: "Abraham, who rejoiced to see Christ's day, and whose offering of Isaac on the mount foreshadowed His death on the cross, and Moses, who wrote of Him, tell me, is the Christ in whom you, Abraham, rejoiced, and of whom you, Moses, wrote, the one in whom I have put my trust?" And with one voice they answer, Abraham from Mount Moriah, and Moses from Mount Sinai, "He is the same!"

I will go to David, and I will ask him: "David, greatest sinner and greatest saint of the Old Testament, is the Christ whose kingdom you said would be an everlasting kingdom, and would stretch from sea to sea and from the river unto the ends of the earth, the Christ in whom I have put my trust?" And with all the music of the psalms, with every string in that marvelous harp pouring out its matchless melody, David answers, "He is the same!"

To whom else can I go? I will go to Isaiah, and I will ask him: "Isaiah, that suffering and triumphant Christ whose portrait you painted, who was wounded for my transgressions and bruised for my iniquities, who was numbered with the transgressors, and yet who shall divide the spoil with the strong and see of the travail of his soul and be satisfied, is He the Christ in whom I have put my trust?" And with his wild, seraphic eloquence Isaiah answers, "He is the same!" I will go to John the Baptist, and I will ask him: "Great forerunner, is the Christ whom you saw that day passing by, and said of Him, 'Behold the Lamb of God, which taketh away the sin of the world,' the Christ whom I trust has taken away my sin?" And with his wild, wilderness voice John answers, "He is the same!"

I will go to Paul, and I will ask him: "Paul, that Christ whom you persecuted, against whose disciples you breathed out threatening and slaughter, but who met you one day at the gate of Damascus and said to you, 'Why persecutest thou me?' and turned you from His greatest enemy into His greatest friend, that one for whose sake you counted all else but refuse, and who, you were persuaded, was able to keep that sin which you had committed unto him against that day, and who, you said, stood by you at the very last in that dungeon at Rome—is He the Christ to whom I have committed my soul against that day?" And with his incomparable eloquence Paul answers, "He is the same!"

I will go to John, and I will ask him: "John, disciple whom Jesus loved, and who leaned upon His breast at the supper, and who said His blood cleanseth us from all sin, is He the Christ upon whose breast I have leaned my head?" And with all the thunders of the Apocalypse, John answers, "He is the same!" I will go to Peter, and I will ask him: "Peter, is that Jesus whom you confessed to be the Son of the living God, whom in His hour of trial you cursed and denied, but who turned and looked upon you with such forgiving love that you went out into the night and wept bitterly —is He the Christ whom I too have oft denied, but whose yearning and redeeming look I too have seen, the One in whose restoring grace I trust?" And with that voice, unmistakable among all sinners, saints, angels, and archangels, Peter answers, "He is the same!"

I will go to the thief on the cross, and I will ask him: "You, who at first reviled Him when you hung at His side on the cross, and then, repenting, said to Him, 'Lord, remember me when thou comest into thy Kingdom,' and heard Him answer you, 'Today shalt thou be with me in paradise'—is He the Christ whose voice I believe I shall one day hear saying to me, 'Today shalt thou be with me in paradise'?" And, with the voice with which only the redeemed can speak, the dying but now forever-living thief answers, "He is the same!"

I will leave all the ages behind, and I will ask all the redeemed, all those who have washed their robes and made them white in the blood of the Lamb, and who lift up their songs by the sea of glass mingled with fire: "Is this Christ whom you praise the one to whom I owe my life and breath, and who saves me from the grave?" And in the music of that new song they answer: "Worthy is the Lamb that was slain to receive power, and riches, and wisdom, and strength, and honor, and glory, and blessing."

There, then, is the eternal and triumphant Christ. When we preach Him, we preach to the eternities. This is the Christ for *you* and for *me*. He is the same yesterday. He is the Christ for your yesterday. Have there been failures, mistakes, transgressions? Are there things you would like to forget and have blotted out? Here then is the Christ for your yesterday. Hear what He says: "Though your sins be as scarlet, they shall be as white as snow; though they be red like crimson, they shall be as wool."

He is the same today. He is the Christ for your today. You have your fears, your burdens, your disappointments, your loneliness, your sorrows, your infirmities, your thorns in the flesh or in the spirit. Here is the Christ for that today. He is able! "Cast thy burden upon the Lord." "Come unto me," He says, "and I will give you rest."

He is the same forever. Here is the Christ for your tomorrow. Who can tell about tomorrow? In vain we try to lift the veil that screens tomorrow. That tomorrow is hid from us. But whatever tomorrow brings, wherever tomorrow takes us, into that unknown territory we can pass in safety and in peace, for He will be there to meet us. He has said, "I will never leave thee, nor forsake thee."

There is another phrase that I would be bold enough to add to this great text, for I am sure it was in the mind of him who wrote the text, although he did not give expression to it. And that phrase is this, "For me!" Can you finish the text that way? Will you finish it that way now, if you have never done so before, that way? Will you say with me *now*, "Jesus Christ the same yesterday, and today, and forever, and for *me*"?

14

THE PRECIOUS BLOOD OF CHRIST

Forasmuch as ye know that ye were not redeemed with corruptible things,
as silver and gold, . . . but with the precious blood of Christ (1 Peter 1:18-19).

Our hearts rejoiced during the war at the tidings of victory which came in from fields of battle around the globe. The Axis armies were being conquered and driven from their strongholds. How was it done? Not by proclamations, not by uniformed correspondents, not by entertainers and visitors to the headquarters of the armies. No! The enemy was conquered by the man with a bayonet in his hand, by the man who fought and bled and died. The war was won at the cost of man's most precious possession—blood.

Likewise, God in His war upon sin and evil in the world, and in the heart of man, wins that victory through blood, the precious blood of Christ. John describes the great battle between the devil and his angels and the followers and the disciples of Christ, and says that "they overcame him by the blood of the lamb" (Rev. 12:11).

Blood is the most precious thing in man's body. A man may have a perfectly framed and beautiful body but if it is drained of its blood, then it becomes nothing but a dead body, a clod. The Old Testament instilled an awful reverence for blood. "Whoso sheddeth man's blood, by man shall his blood be shed" (Gen. 9:6). "For the life of the flesh is in the blood" (Lev. 17:11). It is that which connects and holds together man's body and man's soul. If all blood is precious, how much more so the precious blood of Christ.

When the New Testament speaks, as it so often does, and as Christ Himself does, of the blood of Christ, it means, of course, not just that blood that was poured out upon the cross, but what the pouring out of that blood meant, just as it means in any life—that is, the giving of life in the death of Christ. That is what we think of when we speak of the precious blood of Christ. The blood of Christ is a synonym, then, for the gospel, for redemption, for the salvation of the soul. When Moses received the Book of the Law on Mount Sinai, he sprinkled it with the blood of the sacrifices. This is true not only of Moses' part of the Bible, but of the whole Bible. It is a blood-besprinkled Book. A crimson thread runs through the Bible from the very beginning up to the cross of Christ, and from the cross of Christ to the throne of the Lamb of God. The first greeting that Christ received was that which hailed the power of His blood, when John the Baptist cried out, "Behold the Lamb of God, which taketh away the sin of the world" (John 1:29), and the last salutation that Christ will receive will be the song of the redeemed, "Unto him that loved us, and washed us from our sins in his own blood, . . . be glory and dominion" (Rev. 1:5-6).

Let us see, then, what the Bible says about the wonder-working power of the blood of Christ. We can sum it up, I think, in four great statements. The blood of Christ justifies, redeems, reconciles, and cleanses.

THE BLOOD OF CHRIST JUSTIFIES

In his letter to the Roman Christians Paul said, "Being now justified by his blood." The church dare not abandon, as there is some tendency, the great New Testament words which explain the meaning and power of Christian faith; and here is one of them, this great word "justifies." As the word implies, it means the making just of one who has been unjust. Here the thought is that sin is the breaking of the law, and a broken law demands a penalty. All men, the Bible tells us, have broken the law of God, and in that sense are under the penalty of the law. A holy and just God could not disregard that offense. God could not make light of sin, as many popular salvations do today.

God solved this problem by permitting His only-begotten Son to die for us on the cross. That is, Christ died as our substitute. He died literally in our place. He rendered on our behalf that complete obedience to God's law which was necessary before God could forgive the sinner. Thus God remained just, and yet the justifier of them that believe in Jesus. Man is not merely pardoned and set free from a penalty, but in the power and wisdom and love of God He is made a righteous man. But that could be done only by the precious blood of Christ, poured out on the cross.

Over the portals of a church in Germany there is cut in the stone a beautiful lamb. This is how the lamb happens to be there. A man at work on the steeple of the church lost his footing and plunged to the ground below. A flock of sheep chanced to be grazing in the churchyard, and the fall of the man was broken on a little lamb. The lamb was killed, but the man's life was saved. In his gratitude he cut into the stone over the doors of the church the lamb that saved his life. So we are forgiven and pardoned and saved from the penalty of sin and death by Christ who is the Lamb of God. He, to rescue me from danger, interposed His precious blood.

THE BLOOD OF CHRIST REDEEMS

Christ has many names and titles in the Bible: Lord, Savior, King, Priest, Mediator, the Mighty God, the Prince of Peace. But of all the names which the Bible gives to Jesus, I think Redeemer is the most precious of all. He is the One who has redeemed us; He is our Redeemer. Job said: "I know that my redeemer liveth" (Job 19:25).

Here the thought is that of the bondage and slavery of sin. It is an interesting fact that the influence of Christ's gospel in the world has made it necessary to explain the meaning of the word "redeem." No one needed any such explanation when Peter said that Christ redeemed us. In Peter's day the world was one-half slave. Men were constantly being bought and sold, and that regardless of color. When a man was held in bondage as a slave or as a captive, his family or some kindhearted friend, if he had the means to do so, would redeem the man from slavery with gold or silver or precious stones. That is the meaning that lies back of this great word. Christ paid the price of our redemption. And how great and high the price was! Nothing less than His own precious blood! He came, He said, not to be ministered unto, but to minister, and to lay down His life "a ransom for many." He has redeemed us with an everlasting love.

One of the greatest of English novels, George Eliot's *Romola*, centers around a cultivated Greek, Tito Melema, who, with his father, had been waylaid by pirates in the Mediterranean. When the son managed to escape, the father put into his hands the precious stones with which, when he reached a place of safety, he was to redeem his father from slavery. But the selfish and pleasure-loving son used those precious stones for his own comfort and his own advancement in the world, and forsook and forgot his father who was held in slavery. But how different the act of our faithful friend, our elder brother, who, on the cross, paid the price for our redemption. Now we can trust in His redeeming blood.

In one of the cathedrals of England there lie side by side the effigies of a crusader knight and his lady. But on the effigy of the lady the right hand is wanting. The tradition is that in one of the wars of the Crusades this English knight, fighting under Richard the Lion-Hearted, was taken prisoner. When he besought Saladin, that sometimes magnanimous Moslem conqueror, to set him free and spare his life, for the sake of the love which his lady in England bore him, Saladin scoffed at him, and said that before long she would forget him and marry another. But the knight assured him that she would never do that, but would ever remain faithful.

Saladin asked for a proof of that, and said if the lady would send her right hand as an evidence of her love for her husband, then he would set the knight free. The letter reached the lady in England, who promptly had her right hand cut off and sent to the Moslem conqueror. When Saladin saw it, he set the knight free and sent him back to England. That severed hand was the proof of that lady's devotion to her knight. So the blood of Christ, which was shed for our redemption, is the proof of God's love for us.

THE BLOOD OF CHRIST RECONCILES

Here the thought of man's condition is that of alienation and separation from God. As Isaiah said ages ago: "Your iniquities have separated between you and your God, and your sins have hid his face from you that he will not hear" (Isa. 59:2).

Even in human relationships, wrongdoing produces separation and alienation. The sad records of the divorce courts show how evil-doing separates and alienates those who were once close together. The inevitable tendency of evil-doing, even when it may be covered up and hidden, is to separate the evildoer from the one whom he has wronged. And if that is true between man and man, how true it is between God and man. Yes, sin always alienates, separates, drives out man from the presence of God. Cain sinned and went out from the presence of the Lord. Judas sinned and went out, and it was night. Peter sinned and went out and wept bitterly.

The question, then, is: How can man and God be reconciled? God only knows the answer, and God has given us the answer: By the precious blood of Christ. Perhaps more than anything else, that is what the New Testament says about the blood of Christ, that it makes peace between God and man, that it reconciles man to God. It was to do that great work of reconciliation that Christ came into the world and died upon the cross. That was the peace about which the angels sang when Christ was born, "On earth peace, good will toward men," the peace of reconciliation, the peace of forgiven sin.

Years ago, in a western city, a husband and wife became estranged and parted from one another and, leaving the city where they had lived, went to reside in different parts of the country. Some years afterward the husband chanced to return to this city on a matter of business. When he had concluded his business, he went out to the cemetery where their only son was buried. As he was standing by the grave in tender reminiscence and memory, he heard a step on the gravel behind him and, turning, saw his estranged wife, who had come on the same errand. For the moment the inclination of both was to turn away. But in another moment they thought better of it. Realizing that they had common, binding interest in that grave, instead of turning away, they clasped hands over the dust of their son and were reconciled one to the other. It took nothing less than death to reconcile them. It takes nothing less than the death of Christ, His precious blood, to reconcile man to God.

THE BLOOD OF CHRIST CLEANSES

At first that seems a strange paradox. How could blood cleanse? Blood makes a stain which is deep and distinct, and which every evildoer dreads to leave behind him. Blood has always been the stain and evidence of guilt. But here is the great paradox. The blood of Christ, instead of staining, washes out the stain of sin! Instead of defiling, it washes white the soul of the believer!

More than the guilt of sin, more than the slavery of sin, more than the separation of sin, the awakened conscience feels the stain of sin and the shame of it. The immortal soul, beautiful in itself, and created in the image of God, has been stained with evil. "Sin had left a crimson stain." Yet this is the wonder-working power of the blood of Christ—it has the power to cleanse from the stain of sin. So John said long ago, "The blood of Jesus Christ his Son cleanseth us from all sin" (1 John 1:7).

According to the old legend, Joseph of Arimathea, who took the body of Christ down from the cross, carried the vessel, the Holy Grail, in which he had caught the blood, to Glastonburg, where you can still see the ruins of the cathedral on an island in Somerset. There he formed the order of knights whose duty it was to protect the precious blood. The chief of these knights was made their king. At certain seasons the king unveiled the golden cup which held the precious blood. Then glorious and radiant light fell on the faces of all the knights and endued them with strength from on high. But only the pure in heart could look upon that cup and behold the light which streamed from the blood of Christ.

A beautiful story, it has played a great part in the song and poetry of our race. But, thank God, it is different with that precious blood of Christ in which we put our trust. Only the pure in heart could look upon the Holy Grail. But as for the blood of Christ, as it is presented in the New Testament, the sinner can look upon it and be made clean. "Though your sins be as scarlet, they shall be as white as snow; though they be red like crimson, they shall be as wool" (Isa. 1:18).

> There is a fountain filled with blood
> Drawn from Emmanuel's veins;

And sinners, plunged beneath that flood,
  Lose all their guilty stains.

How great, then, the wonder-working power of the precious blood of Christ upon the souls of those who in faith receive Him and trust in Him! A British general, Hedley Vicars, waiting one day at his quarters for another officer to come in and see him, began to leaf through a Bible that lay on his desk. His eye fell on those words of John, "The blood of Jesus Christ his Son cleanseth us from all sin." Closing the book he said: "If this is true, henceforth I will live, by the grace of God, as a man should live who has been washed in the blood of Christ." Yes, if that is true, that for you and me the precious blood of Christ has been shed, then how we ought to live for Him!

John Milton used to say that the greatness and sacredness of man's soul is attested by two facts: first, the creation of his soul in the image of the eternal God; and second, the price that had been paid for the redemption of his soul, even the precious blood of Christ. Will you live up to that great fact? Will you follow Him who has redeemed you with the precious blood of Christ, as of a lamb without spot and without blemish?

15

A GOOD CONSCIENCE

The answer of a good conscience toward God   (1 Peter 3:21).

The Commercial Airlines of the United States transport hundreds of thousands of passengers millions of flying miles each year with very few disasters. This achievement is due in part to that remarkable device known as the radio beam. The beam is not, as its name might seem to imply, a beam of light, but a path of radio waves emanating from the sending station and spreading out at its greatest width over five miles. When a plane veers off that radio path to the right, the pilot gets the signal "N," or dash and dot. When he veers off to the left, he gets the signal "A," or dot and dash. When he is directly on the beam he hears a constant hum, and when he is immediately over the landing field there is a zone of silence. Thus through rain and snow and storm and fog and night's blackness the great ships are able to carry their passengers to the desired haven. A wonderful triumph of man's inventive genius, and a marvelous conquest of the laws of nature! But within the breast of each living man and woman is something more wonderful and more mysterious than that radio beam. It is that beam of divine light and guidance which we call *conscience*.

Conscience is the most wonderful thing in man. The author of *The Critique of Pure Reason*, Immanuel Kant, said there were just two things that filled him with awe—the starry heavens and conscience in the breast of man. Conscience is the sufficient proof of God—who is the Author of it—of the soul, and of the hereafter.

Conscience is our wisest counselor and teacher, our most faithful and most patient friend, and—our worst enemy. There are no rewards comparable to the rewards of conscience. There are no punishments so severe and inexorable as those of conscience. The "well done" of conscience is our purest joy, its condemnation our deepest misery.

There is a beautiful verse in the book of Proverbs which reads: "The spirit of man is the candle of the Lord" (Prov. 20:27). Another and a clearer rendering is Dr. Moffatt's: "Man's conscience is the lamp of the Eternal." Conscience is God's lamp in man's breast. Now and then we hear of attempts to explain away or dispense with conscience. But conscience is supremely heedless of that. It goes on bestowing its rewards and inflicting its punishments. In his "The Island" Lord Byron wrote:

> Yet still there whispers the small voice within,
> Heard through gain's silence, and o'er glory's din:
> Whatever creed he taught or land he trod,
> Man's conscience is the oracle of God.

THE GUIDANCE, INSTRUCTION, AND WARNING OF CONSCIENCE

In *Paradise Lost*, at the creation of man, Milton puts into the mouth of the Creator these words: "I will put mine umpire, Conscience, in his breast." There is the shortest and best definition of conscience ever made. The umpire calls the play, whether it is fair or foul. So conscience calls the thought, the word, the deed, whether it is right or wrong.

The ancients talked of a magic ring which had the appearance of any other ring, yet was possessed of extraordinary qualities. Whenever an evil thought passed through the mind of him who wore the ring, or whenever he was tempted to do an evil deed, the ring pressed painfully upon his finger. Yet each one of us wears a ring more wonderful than that fabled magic ring of the ancients, and that is the magic ring of conscience. A man may or may not obey, but conscience faithfully does its part.

The Bible, that greatest book of illustrations, in a vivid and dramatic way makes clear this power of conscience to instruct and guide and warn. At the very beginning of time, the tempter came to the woman and told her that what God had said was not true, and that if she ate of the tree of the knowledge of good and evil she would not die, but become as a god, knowing good and evil. Immediately conscience flashed its warning and she repeated to the tempter the words of God: "Ye shall not eat of it, neither shall ye touch it, lest ye die" (Gen. 3:3). Let no one think that this part of the Bible is outmoded. It is the most modern page in the Bible. The history recorded there has been re-enacted and repeated today in some social parlor, in a quiet study, on a crowded street, in a business office, or in a country lane. There temptation has spoken its seductive whisper, and there conscience has flashed its warning and has been obeyed or disobeyed to the lasting good or the lasting hurt of the soul.

Take the case of Joseph, that timeless character for young men and young women. In the hour of his great temptation everything seemed to be on the side of his yielding to it: the hot impulses of youth, the flattery of a great woman, the desire for preferment in Egypt, the dread of incurring the wrath of this woman if he scorned her proposal, than which hell hath no greater fury. And yet Joseph won his victory. He obeyed conscience. He said, "How then can I do this great wickedness, and sin against God?" (Gen. 39:9). Therefore it is that forty centuries after he lived, and in a part of the world not then known to be in existence, Joseph's character and his battle are held up as an example of how to live.

Take the case of Pilate. What a battle of conscience that was! The moment Jesus stood before his judgment seat in the gray light of that early morning, Pilate knew that Jesus was an innocent and righteous man. The verdict of his own conscience was strikingly confirmed by the dream of his wife, who sent him her message: "Have thou nothing to do with that just man: for I have suffered many things this day in a dream because of him" (Matt. 27:19). This double verdict was confirmed by a private examination of Jesus. Pilate struggled hard to obey conscience and do nothing against Jesus. When he heard that He was from Galilee, Pilate thought he could rid himself of the responsibility by handing him over to the jurisdiction of Herod.

But Herod mocked Him and set Him at nought and sent Him back to Pilate. Then Pilate proposed to the people that Jesus be the one chosen that year for the governor's clemency. But they shouted their preference for a murderer and a robber, Barabbas.

Then Pilate had Jesus scourged, and brought Him out bleeding from His wounds and exposed Him to the mob, saying, "Behold the man!" (John 19:5), hoping that this would satisfy them. But they shouted all the louder, "Crucify him, crucify him." Still Pilate hesitated; still he had not given up the battle.

Then, from the back of the crowd, someone with a raucous voice cried out, "If thou let this man go, thou art not Caesar's friend" (John 19:12). That ended the battle. When Pilate heard that "not Caesar's friend," he thought of his patron, the gloomy Tiberius; he thought of his high office, his villas, his chariots, the pleasures of his life. "Thou art not Caesar's friend." That ended the battle. Pilate surrendered. That is always a tragedy when the soul refuses the voice of conscience and obeys instead the voice of the mob, the voice of expediency, the voice of the lower nature, the voice of time, rather than the voice of eternity.

These illustrations are sufficient to show how conscience instructs and warns. God permits no one to take the path of evil without that inner warning. Conscience never deceives. It will never connive at irregularity or deviation from the right. What would you think of an airline pilot who got one of those warning signals, dash-dot or dot-dash—that he was off the beam—and paid no attention to it? And yet how many there are who are in command, not of a million-dollar plane, but of an immortal soul, worth the precious blood of Christ, who receive the faithful, solemn warning of conscience and pay no heed to it!

> Then keep thy conscience sensitive,
>   No inward token miss;
> And go where grace entices thee,
>   Thy safety lies in this.

The president of one of our Eastern universities summoned a young man before him on charges of misconduct. He asked him to explain his action and defend it as best he could. The young man did so, and as he finished he said: "Why, Mr. President, there are not ten men in this university who would not have done as I did!"

The president looked at him, and said quietly, "Young man, did it never occur to you that you might have been one of those ten?"

Life calls each one of us to the select company of those who live in loyalty to conscience: "Be loyal to the royal in yourself."

This is the thrill of preaching, and of preaching on a theme like this—that the preacher's words may coincide with some battle of conscience in the soul of the one to whom he is speaking. One Sunday evening, unknown to me, sat a young woman, home over the weekend from college. She was facing a dangerous temptation and had not yet decided to say, "No." I was speaking of the warnings we get from the voice of God and the importance of obeying that voice. A few days later I received a letter from the young woman in which she wrote:

"When I shook hands with you after the service at the foot of the gallery stairs I spoke some platitudes about how I enjoyed the sermon. But that was not what I was feeling. That was not what I was thinking. That was not what I was saying to myself. What I was saying to myself was this, 'Now, get this! It's wrong, and you are not going to do it.'"

THE CONDEMNATION AND PUNISHMENT OF CONSCIENCE

The engineer of a train or the pilot of a ship or a plane who disregards a warning signal pays the consequence in disaster for himself and others. The natural law makes no excuse. Neither does the moral law. Neither does conscience. No bribe and no threat and no tears can suspend its judgment or revoke its sentence. No immersion in business or pleasure can hush the voice of conscience or protect the soul from its judgments or pluck its sting.

What are some of the punishments of conscience? One of these is *the loss of joy*, the unrest of the soul. This is perhaps the saddest punishment of all, for man was created for joy. The morning stars sang together over his creation, and all the sons of God shouted for joy. But the sense of guilt, the reproach of conscience, withers the leaves of the tree of happiness, takes all satisfaction out of the highest achievement, and turns the acclaim and recognition of men into bitterness.

The post office in every metropolitan city has what is called a "Conscience Fund." This contains money returned to the post office by those who had in some way defrauded the government. In many cases the money was sent back long after the commission of the theft and when there was no likelihood of apprehension or arrest. It was not the fear of arrest or the fear of punishment that made the evildoer send back the money, but the reproach of his conscience, with the resultant unhappiness and unrest.

It was the commencement day at one of our great universities. The commencement address had been delivered, the diplomas granted, and the honorary degrees conferred. The president then said to the throng present in the commencement hall that he had an important announcement to make. Everyone was on the alert to see or hear what it would be. Perhaps it would be some great gift to the university, or some new field of learning which was to be opened up, or some distinction which had come to a member of the faculty.

But it was none of these. The president said that some weeks before the commencement he had received a letter from a prominent alumnus in which he said that he was returning his diploma to the university because he had cheated in his final examination in his senior year. He now felt that he was unworthy of the diploma thus dishonestly gained, and said that his conscience would not permit him to retain it. The president had written him, telling him that he appreciated his sense of honor in the matter and his recognition of a high moral standard; but that the useful and honorable life which he had led since he left the university atoned in a way for his mistake and transgression, and he asked him to let him return to him his diploma. But the man answered that his conscience would not permit him to take it back since it had been dishonestly secured. Then, amid a silence which could be felt, the president held up the diploma and said, "Here is the diploma, but with the name cut out." The hundreds in the graduating class that day and the multitude in the commencement hall heard a lesson on conscience and its punishments which none of them could forget to their dying hour.

Another punishment of conscience is *fear*. After the man and the woman in the Garden of Eden had disobeyed conscience and broken the law of God and then heard the voice of God walking in the garden, they were afraid and hid themselves amid the trees of the garden. There again the first book of the Bible is the most modern in the world. What the man and the woman did when they hid themselves in the garden, thousands upon thousands have done this day. What made them afraid? Who told them they were naked? What, but conscience? "Thus conscience does make cowards of us all."

Theodoric the Ostrogoth, greatest of the Gothic kings, ruled at Ravenna for thirty-three years, at the end of the fifth century and in the first quarter of the sixth century. At Ravenna, on the Adriatic, where one can see the tomb of Dante also, is the great mausoleum of Theodoric. A chapel in circular form is crowned by a dome of one entire piece of granite. From the center of the dome arise four columns which support in a porphyry vase the remains of the great king, surrounded by the bronze statues of the twelve apostles. The last years of the illustrious reign of Theodoric were stained by his murder of the patrician Symmachus and the noble Boethius, the "last of the Romans," and author of *The Consolations of Philosophy*, written in the tower of Pavia as he was awaiting the stroke of death. By the mandate of Theodoric, Boethius was strangled with a cord, till his eyes almost burst from their sockets. As he himself was now descending to the grave, Theodoric's conscience was tortured with remorse and alarmed by the unknown terrors of the future. At the royal table one night the head of a large fish was served. As he looked upon the head of that fish, the king cried out that he saw the countenance of one of those two men whom he had murdered, his mouth armed with devouring teeth and his eyes glaring with fury and revenge. Trembling with chill and cold, Theodoric was conducted to his bedchamber, where, under a weight of bedclothes, he expressed to his physician his repentance for the murders of Boethius and Symmachus. In a few days the king was dead. Only the head of a fish! And yet the vision of that fish smote the soul of the great king with the pangs of remorse.

Conscience driven away as a friend and counselor comes back in the form of remorse:

> "Good-bye," I said to my conscience;
>   "Good-bye for aye and aye";
> And I put her hands off harshly,
>   And turned my face away.
> And conscience, smitten sorely,
>   Returned not from that day.

But a time came when my spirit
    Grew weary of its pace,
And I cried, "Come back, my conscience,
    I long to see thy face."
But conscience cried, "I cannot.
    Remorse sits in my place!"

Is God too good to punish, and to punish in the future? Men sometimes debate this question. We pass by the answer for a moment. But as we do so we observe that whether God is, or is not, too good to punish, man certainly is not. Within his own breast he carries all the instruments and agents of suffering and retribution, "Their worm shall not die, neither shall their fire be quenched" (Isa. 66:24).

A man had a wolf cub which grew up with him like one of his children, drank out of his own cup, and lay on his own breast. But one day, when the cub had become a full-grown wolf, the call of the wild came back upon him. When the man opened the door one day there stood the wolf, its tail extended, its bristles upright, its eyes blazing, its fangs unbared. When men who heard the man's cries had beaten off the wolf and rescued the mutilated woodsman and put him to bed, he exclaimed: "Thank God I have been torn by the fangs of a wolf and not by the fangs of conscience!"

THE REWARDS OF CONSCIENCE

There are no rewards like the rewards of conscience; no honorary degree, Doctor of Divinity, Doctor of Letters, Doctor of Laws, can compare with the "well done" of a man's conscience. No military decoration, the Victoria Cross, the Congressional Medal, can compare with the reward of a good conscience. In the time of tribulation or persecution or slander there is no friend like the answer of a good conscience. This answer may involve sacrifice and suffering, but it always pays a high dividend.

Joseph had to pay a high price to be faithful to his conscience. Because he said "No" to the temptress he was cast into the dungeon. I wonder if that first night in the dungeon some tempting voice or Spirit said to him: "Joseph, you are a fool. If only you had said 'Yes' instead of 'No,' you might have been riding around in Potiphar's chariot today, instead of lying here in this stinking dungeon!" But do you remember what comes next in that great narrative? Even in prison "the Lord was with him." And the Lord always is with all those who are true to conscience. Soon Joseph was out of the prison, and Pharaoh's gold chain was about his neck. That same golden chain is forged by the angels for everyone who is true to God.

The greatest story of loyalty to conscience is that of those three Hebrew lads at Babylon who, when commanded to bow down to Nebuchadnezzar's golden image, rendered their immortal answer: "Our God whom we serve is able to deliver us from the burning fiery furnace . . . but if not, be it known unto thee, O king, that we will not serve thy gods, worship the golden image which thou hast set up" (Dan. 3:17-18). What they said was: "We will burn to cinders, but we will not deny our God or bow down to your image!" Into the furnace, heated seven times hotter than usual, they were flung. But when the conscience-stricken Nebuchadnezzar went to look into the furnace, he cried out in astonishment to his counselors: "Did not we cast three men bound into the midst of the fire? . . . Lo, I see four men loose, walking in the midst of the fire, and they have no hurt; and the form of the fourth is like the Son of God" (Dan. 3:24-25). Yes, that is it! The form of the fourth! And the form of the fourth, the Son of God, will go into the hottest furnace with those who remain true to Him.

When John Bunyan was in Bedford jail he was offered release upon condition that he would promise not to preach the gospel on the streets. It was a great temptation to him, especially when he thought of his wife and children, and above all, of his blind daughter, Mary. "O my poor blind one," he would say to himself, "what sorrows thou art likely to have in this life; and now I cannot so much as endure the thought that the wind should blow upon thee!" But then Bunyan thought of God, he thought of his soul, and gave his great answer: "Unless I am willing to make my conscience a continual slaughtershop and butchery, then, God Almighty being my witness, the moss shall grow upon these eyebrows before I surrender my principles or violate my conscience!"

Bunyan was therefore well qualified to write that noble passage on conscience in *Pilgrim's Progress*, how, when Mr. Honest, receiving his summons to go over the river, came down to find that it overflowed all its banks. But, long before, he had made an appointment with one Good Conscience to meet him there, and help him over the river, "the which he did, and so helped him over."

That is what we all ought to do—make an appointment with our conscience, who will meet us at every river or trial and so help us over. John B. Minor was the distinguished dean of the law school at the University of Virginia for many years. The subject upon which he lectured in the school was real property. It was his custom to say at the end of the last lecture to every senior class: "Remember, young men, the most valuable property any man can possess is a commending conscience."

But whose conscience is altogether good? Whose conscience can render a perfect answer? We have seen what conscience can do, and how mighty it is, how it can guide and instruct and warn and punish and bless. But there is one thing conscience cannot do. It cannot revoke its sentence or suspend its judgment. It cannot heal the wound which it inflicts. It cannot wash out the stain from the soul. It cannot undo the past. It cannot cover up the transgression, for its business is not to cover up, but to *uncover*. Hence it is that we all need the great mercy of God in Christ, whose blood cleanses us from all sin. He alone can say to conscience, "Be still!" Come, then, to the foot of the cross, the cross where Paul, who persecuted Christ, found peace; where Peter, who denied Him, found peace; and where the thief, who reviled Him, found peace— that peace of God which passeth all understanding. "Though your sins be as scarlet, they shall be as white as snow" (Isa. 1:18).

16

SILENCE IN HEAVEN

And when he had opened the seventh seal, there was silence in heaven about the space of half an hour (Revevation 8:1).

When a door was opened in heaven to John, he saw a great white throne girt about with a rainbow. Out of the throne proceeded lightnings and thunders and voices; and the seven lamps, which are the seven Spirits of God, burned on every side. Before the throne rolled a sea of glass, and around the throne were the four living creatures with the face of the lion, the ox, the eagle, and the man. Upon the throne sat the holy one, and in his hand was a book sealed with seven seals.

With a loud voice, a strong angel cried out: "Who is worthy to open the book, and to loose the seals thereof?" (Rev. 5:2). John waited anxiously for someone to answer the challenge and the invitation. But none in heaven, none of the great angels or archangels, and no man on earth, none of the sages and philosophers, was worthy to open the book, or even to look upon its sealed and mystic contents. John wept much that none was found worthy to read the book and to look upon it. But as he wept, he beheld a strange sight. In the midst of the throne and of the four living creatures stood a Lamb as it had been slain. The Lamb came and took the book out of the right hand of him that sat upon the throne. At this, the living creatures and all about the throne fell down before the Lamb, ascribing unto him majesty and dominion. And all the angels, ten thousand times ten thousand, took up the chorus, in which every living creature in heaven and on earth joined, "Worthy is the Lamb that was slain. Blessing, and honor, and glory, and power, be unto him that sitteth upon the throne, and unto the Lamb forever and ever" (Rev. 5:12, 13).

Taking the book, the Lamb broke the first of the seven seals. There was a crash of thunder, and John saw a white horse going forth to battle. The warrior who sat upon him had a crown on his head and a bow in his hand, and went forth conquering and to conquer. This was a symbol of the victory of Christ and the church. The second seal was broken, and behold, a red horse came forth, and he that sat upon the horse had power to take peace from the earth, and in his hand was a great sword. This was war. The church will triumph, but she will have tribulation. Wherever she delivers her true message, she will meet with opposition and antagonism.

Then the Lamb broke the third seal, and lo, a black horse galloped forth. In the hand of the rider was a pair of balances, and a voice proclaimed: "A measure of wheat for a penny, and three measures of barley for a penny" (Rev. 6:6). This was famine, which should scourge the earth.

The fourth seal was opened, and behold, a pale horse, and his name that sat on him was Death, and Hell followed with him, and power was given unto Death to kill with the sword and with hunger and with death and with the beasts of the earth. Then the fifth seal was broken, and under the altar of God John saw the souls of them that were slain for the Word of God. These were the martyrs, crying with a loud voice: "How long, O Lord, holy and true, dost thou not judge and avenge our blood on them that dwell on the earth?" (Rev. 6:10). Their cry was answered, and they were clothed in white, waiting for the completion of the whole number, the noble army of the martyrs who have laid down their lives for Christ.

Then the sixth seal was broken. The sun became black as sackcloth, the moon became as blood, the stars fell from heaven, and the earth shook with an earthquake. And all the kings of the earth, and all men of every station, down to the lowest slave, hid themselves, and said to the mountains and the rocks: "Fall on us, and hide us from the face of him that sitteth on the throne, and from the wrath of the Lamb" (Rev. 6:16). This was a picture of the commotions and judgments which shall accompany the advent of Christ.

Then the Lamb broke the remaining seal, the seventh. And "there was silence in heaven about the space of half an hour" (Rev. 8:1). At the opening of the first seal there was a crash of thunder; and when the succeeding seals were broken, a great voice cried to John, "Come and see." But now there is silence. No roll of thunder, no voice like the sound of many waters, no proclamation of doom and no benediction of mercy. The waves of time have ceased to break upon time's shore, and even the river of the water of life is still. No cry of the souls of the martyrs for justice is heard from beneath the altar, no groans of the oppressed, nor sobs of the impenitent, nor songs of the redeemed, but silence. Silence in heaven, silence upon earth.

There is nothing so impressive as silence. I like to wander into some great cathedral and, standing alone in the nave, listen to the silence of the immense pillars, the soaring arches, and the angels and the saints carved upon the pillars or looking down upon me from the windows.

Nature too has great silences. The sea is magnificent when it is broken and driven by the lash of the wind. But it is still grander and more mysterious when it lies under the ship without a wave, motionless as a sea of glass. The mountains are noble in their silence, and so is the forest when not a leaf stirs beneath the wind. The cedars of Lebanon sometimes, with their gigantic arms like vast harps, respond to the breath of the wind and throw out music like the breaking of the waves on the shore of the distant sea. But still more impressive are they when they stand silent and motionless, the sad and lonely survivors of the generations which have passed over them.

Then there is the silence of wonder and expectation. In his well-known poem "On First Looking into Chapman's Homer" John Keats says he felt

> like stout Cortez, when with eagle eyes
> He stared at the Pacific—and all his men
> Looked at each other with a wild surmise—
> Silent, upon a peak in Darien.

There is the silence of affection, the love which requires for its expression no spoken word. There is the silence of guilt, when, under the accusation of wrongdoing, the guilty soul offers no excuse. And last of all there is the deep silence of death, a silence which is one of the most familiar and common of all the things we meet in this life, and yet as mysterious as when Cain first looked upon bleeding, dead, and silent Abel.

But what a silence was this, the silence which prevailed in heaven for the space of half an hour! It was not the silence of expectation, nor the silence with which guilt hears the decree of its punishment, nor the silence with which men wait for the appearance of another event on the slowly turning wheel of fate. It was the silence which marked the achievement of the destiny of the human race, the complete unfolding and vindication of the plan and purpose of God, the finish of the work of redemption. Then all is silent. There is no complaint, no protest, no question to ask. War and hatred and strife and sin have passed away.

GOD'S PLAN

This silence which John heard in heaven, more impressive than all its voices and all its thunders, tells us, first of all, that God has a plan and a purpose which He is working out in this world and through men. The seven-sealed book, which the Lamb alone could take and open, is the book which contains the history of the world and the destiny of mankind. As the successive seals are loosed, the visions which appear illustrate the history of the world—its chapters of blood and violence, and its returning tides of judgment and woe as God judges men through their own vices; the wars and famines and pestilences which scourge the earth; the courage, the patience, the endurance, the suffering and the triumphs of the good. All this goes out before us in the sublime and awful panorama which the apostle saw unrolled at Patmos' sea-beat rock. But at the end, as at the beginning, God is on the throne, and the disorder and strife and confusion of time issue finally in the deep and beautiful silence of the Kingdom of God.

Profitable for believers at all times, this picture and apocalypse has a particular meaning for our own age and our own time, when there is so much conflict, such confused counsel, and when no human voice can tell what a day may bring forth. At such a time we do well to listen to the silence which comes at the end of the plan and the purpose of God. Alarmed and troubled by the voices which clash so fiercely about us, we find strength and assurance when we turn from this troubled scene and listen to the silence which is in heaven.

In a great battle, with the smoke rising along its far-flung lines, and the earth shaking with the noise of the artillery, a man coming suddenly upon the scene might conclude that it meant nothing, and that no plan or schedule of battle was being worked out. But in reality what appears to be a scene of confusion and chaos and accident is the arena upon which is being worked out a plan and a method and a purpose, every detail of which is ordered and governed by the commanding general. So the history of the world, and the condition of the world today, may seem to you and me nothing but a field of meaningless chaos, confusion, and violence. But it is not so to the all-seeing eye of Him who holds the nations in the hollow of His hand, who has determined beforehand their times and seasons, who is making the wrath of man to praise Him, and day by day and age by age is working out His almighty purpose.

In a sermon preached in Pittsburgh in the Third Presbyterian Church, April 23, 1865, at the time of Lincoln's assassination, on the text, "How unsearchable are his judgments, . . . for of him, and through him, and to him, are all things: to whom be glory forever," the distinguished preacher, Dr. Herrick Johnson, said:

"That God reigns, that in the government of human affairs He has a plan, and that the accomplishment of that plan is by judgments unsearchable and ways past finding out—ways not ours, and of which we have had no thought or conception until their revelation has struck men dumb with astonishment and bewildering wonder—are truths emphasized and corroborated with remarkable frequency and remarkable power ever since the outbreak of the Civil War. We of the North sought to lay the strong hand of the government upon this petty revolt and crush it in ninety days. God's way was to soak our land with gore and redden our rivers with blood and thicken the very air with groans for four long years before we should subdue it."

CHRIST IS GOD'S PLAN

Not only has God revealed that He has a plan, that time's drama is His drama, and that all nations and all men are but the brief embodiment or the transient realization of that plan, but He has revealed that this plan centers in His Son, the Lord Jesus Christ. It was the Lamb of God who alone could break the seals of the book in which was written the history of the world and the destiny of the race. That history and that destiny is fulfilled in Christ, who is set to be a prince and a ruler. He was the rider with the crown upon His head who went forth conquering and to conquer.

The church must own and worship the complete and full-orbed Christ—not merely the Christ whose words lead us into truth, whose example lights our path through life, and whose presence stills our pain and makes our peace, but the Christ in whom the great purposes of God for the world are being worked out, who is the alpha and the omega, the beginning and the end of history, who holds in His hands judgments and blessings. However little today the world may own or obey that Christ, He is the only leader, the King of Kings and Lord of Lords.

GOD AND YOUR LIFE

In the silence which reigned for half an hour in heaven, and which tells of the victorious completion and universal acceptance of God's plan for the world, there is the promise of peace and hope for the individual also. We have been talking about God in history, a grand theme. But we close now with something else, God in providence, God in your life and in mine. If God rules in the armies of heaven, He also draws near to you and me. If His infinite intelligence can tell the number of the stars, His tender compassion can also heal the brokenhearted. How much there is in life which will sometimes make the heart to ache and the mind to stagger! "Why?" is the question which is so often upon our lips. "I remembered God," each of us says with the psalmist, "and was troubled" (77:3).

Here we have the assurance that, although we cannot answer our own questions, God has the answer; that at the end, when all has been made clear, there will be no complaint, no appeal, and no protest against the ways of God. I remember a well-known minister telling one day in a sermon an anecdote of his boyhood days concerning his older brother, also a distinguished preacher of the gospel. The older brother was clever with his jackknife, and could contrive and carve what to the younger boy were wonderful objects. When he was first working on the stick of wood, the impatient younger brother would tease him to tell what he was going to make. Always the brother with the knife would say, "Wait until I get through."

Wait until God gets through with your life. Then you will wonder at what He has done, and how He has done it. Then there will be no complaints, no protests, and no tearful questionings. "In that day ye shall ask me nothing." There will be silence in heaven, silence in your heart and in mine, the deep, deep silence of grateful wonder, glad acceptance, and everlasting praise. Then we shall be able to sing:

> With mercy and with judgment,
>   My web of time He wove,
> And aye the dews of sorrow
>   Were lustered with His love.
> I'll bless the hand that guided,
>   I'll bless the heart that planned,
> When throned where glory dwelleth
>   In Immanuel's land.

"O the depth of the riches both of the wisdom and knowledge of God! How unsearchable are his judgments, and his ways past finding out!" (Rom. 11:33).

17

BEHOLD, A WHITE HORSE

*And I saw heaven opened, and behold, a white horse; and he that sat
upon him was called Faithful and True*   (Revelation 19:11).

Milan, a famous city on the Lombard Plain, is a place of stirring memories. In the ruins of the church of St. Ambrogio you recall how Ambrose there refused Theodosius the sacrament because of his massacre of the populace at Thessalonica. When the emperor protested, by way of extenuation, that David was both a murderer and an adulterer, Ambrose said to him, "You have imitated David in his crime; now imitate him in his repentance."

One's heart thrills to remember that under that same blue sky, and perhaps on the very spot over which one is walking, the Holy Spirit won His mighty conquest over the soul of Augustine.

In the refectory of the monastery of Santa Maria della Grazie you can see the poor ghost of Leonardo da Vinci's "Last Supper." But the chief glory of Milan is its cathedral. Coming out of the glare of the Italian sun, you find the great spaces of Europe's third largest cathedral, and in some respects its most beautiful, stretching out before you. The 52 marble columns which hold up the lofty octagonal dome, and the 4,440 turrets, pinnacles, and the statues of angels and saints produce an incomparable combination of grace and grandeur, beauty and vastness.

Passing behind the high altar, you are suddenly confronted by one of the largest stained-glass windows in the world, like a window opened in heaven. The afternoon sun streaming through the window turns it into a sea of glass mingled with fire, whereon are depicted, not the scenes of the Old Testament, the Creation, the Fall, the Flood, Abraham, Jacob, Joseph, Moses, Elijah, David, the judges, the kings, and the prophets; nor the scenes of the Gospels, the Incarnation, the Temptation, the Denial, the Transfiguration, the Betrayal, the Crucifixion, the Resurrection, and the Ascension; nor scenes from the Acts, the preaching of the apostles and the spread of the gospel; but the tremendous imagery of the Apocalypse—the sounding trumpets, the outpoured vials, Michael and his angels in battle with the dragon and his angels, the star Wormwood falling out of heaven, the great angel with the rainbow upon his head, standing with one foot on the sea and the other on the earth, and swearing by Him that liveth forever and ever that time shall be no longer, the woman clothed with the sun and the moon under her feet, Satan bound with a chain and cast into the bottomless pit, the Great White Throne, and the white horse and his rider going forth to conquer, with the armies of heaven in his train.

There are things in the book of Revelation which we cannot understand and about which we cannot be sure, but there are many things that we can understand. When you behold the fall of Babylon, lamented on earth and celebrated in heaven, when you see the overthrow of the false prophet and the beast and the dragon, when you behold the white horse and his rider, his vesture dipped in blood, with many crowns upon his head, and on his vesture and on his thigh a name written—King of Kings and Lord of Lords—you know that what you are beholding is the victory of the Kingdom of Christ.

Come then with me into this glorious cathedral of our faith, and with the lights and tumults of the world shut out let us contemplate the triumph of Christ. Let us behold first the certainty of the triumph of Christ and the necessity of an invincible faith in that triumph, and second how that triumph will come through Christ, by Christ, and for Christ alone.

THE CERTAINTY OF THE TRIUMPH

When the seamen that night on Paul's shipwrecked vessel knew that they were driving toward some shore, they must have wondered just how that voyage was going to end. So we wonder about the end of the world drift, the end of world history. "Then cometh the end" was the great utterance of the apostle Paul.

The end is just as logical and inevitable as the beginning. All objects and processes of nature, as we behold them, have not only a beginning but an ending. The day dawns, the sun runs his course and sinks beyond the horizon, and the day is ended. The night begins. The moon and the stars come up. At length they fade and disappear. The shadows depart, the day begins to dawn. The night is ended.

The tiny rivulet begins to flow high up on the mountain ridge and becomes the great river which blesses the earth with its waters. At length the river loses itself in the ocean. The river has come to an end.

The Bible, and the Bible alone, tells us of a great and glorious end to human history. It is there that we see the great movement toward righteousness reaching its climax in the Kingdom of God. The splendor of that climax is reflected in the book of Revelation, and nowhere is that splendor more overcoming than in this vision of the white horse and his rider, with the armies of heaven in his train.

In his great sermon on "Suffering for Christ" John Calvin said: "All the exhortations which can be given us to suffer for the name of Jesus Christ and in defense of the gospel, will have no effect if we do not feel sure of the cause for which we fight." That assurance of the victory of our cause is granted to us in the Apocalypse. This vision of victory is necessary for our faith and endurance and hope. You and I in our day see too little and, at the same time, too much, and often what we do see seems stronger than what we believe. Hence we must have the supplement of the book of Revelation, where we see the triumph of the truth and principles which are elsewhere declared in the Scriptures. Thus it is that no preacher has sounded the highest note until he has echoed the trumpet of the Apocalypse. No preacher has stood upon the highest ground till he has stood here and looked down the long corridors of time until those corridors converge in the Kingdom of God. It is here that we see the rainbow which spans the stormy sky of human history, and it is here that we listen to the melodized thunder of the last great day when the kingdoms of this world shall have become the kingdoms of our Lord, and of His Christ—a day so splendid that, compared with it, the brightest day that has hitherto shone upon the world is but midnight, and the fairest splendors which have invested it are but the shadow of darkness.

If this vision of the triumph of Christ was necessary for the church and the Roman Empire when that pagan empire was striving to drown the church in its own blood, it is not less necessary for us today when Antichrist has invented new masks for his face and has multiplied his lies and his perversions of the truth.

> Our Lord is still rejected
>   And by this world disowned;
> By the many still neglected
>   And by the few enthroned.

There are times when the heart grows dull and heavy with the deadly monotony of evil in the world. The origin of evil troubles us. Why did God permit it? We try to answer that by saying that for a moral being there must be the freedom of choice and, therefore, the possibility of evil. The continuance of evil troubles us.

In John's vision the beast, who had received his death stroke and had hid for a time spouting blood, emerged at length from the abyss with his death stroke healed, and the whole world wandered after the beast and worshiped him. So evil in the hearts of men and in human institutions is constantly re-emerging and reincarnating itself, its death stroke healed. We comfort ourselves with the thought that God is able to bring good out of evil, but still we shall ask ourselves: Is God not omnipotent? Is God not all good? And if so, why did He permit evil in the beginning? Why does He not destroy it now?

The great answer that the Bible gives us, and the answer of this vision, is the certainty of the destruction and overthrow of evil. When Robinson Crusoe's man Friday wanted to know why God did not destroy the Devil, the answer that Crusoe finally gave him was the right answer, and the only answer, and the great answer: "God will destroy him."

We see the ebb and flow of progress and decay, the unfolding of the long and bloody panorama of history, humanity's aspiration of the best and its doing of the worst. We see the church in ceaseless battle with the beast. But that is not all we see. Look at this window! Here you see the end of evil—"Then cometh the end."

You see the Lamb of God standing upon Mount Zion. You see all things put under His feet. You see the white horse and his rider, with the armies of heaven in his train and many crowns upon his head. You see this world of strife and toil and envy and hate and sin and passion and blood and death give way to the new heavens and the new earth, wherein dwelleth righteousness, not as a fugitive visitor, but as the eternal and unbroken order.

THE TRIUMPH OF CHRIST

The triumph of righteousness will come for Christ, by Christ, and through Christ alone. People look forward to a golden age, to the triumph of justice and righteousness and the benediction of universal peace. But how will this come about? "Then cometh the end." But by what means will the end come?

It will not come through any natural growth or development. There are those who speak as if they think that is the way by which we shall reach the millennial age. They believe there is a law of irresistible and invincible progress at work in the world and running through the ages. The ape and the tiger will die in humanity. The tide of justice and good will and righteousness will rise higher and higher until the whole earth shall be covered with its flood. They tell us to look back over the past by which the human race has come. Behold the broken fetters which he has cast aside. Behold the bones and skeletons of the systems of iniquity and wickedness which have been overthrown and destroyed. All that humanity needs is time, and progress counts time in aces. Progress takes one step and the ages have elapsed. With progress one day is as a thousand years, and a thousand years as one day.

But this theory, this hypothesis of unstoppable and invincible progress, regardless of what men and nations do, regardless of the moral law, crumbles before fact. This theory received a rude shock in World war I, and World War II almost destroyed it.

If there is progress, there is also retrogression. If there is construction, there is also destruction. The great French entomologist Fabre, after tracing the advance of human knowledge, asks:

"To what an ideal height will this process and evolution lead mankind? To no very magnificent height, it is to be feared. We are afflicted with an indelible taint, a sort of original sin. We are made after a pattern and can do nothing to change ourselves. We are marked with the mark of the beast, the taint of the belly, the inexhaustible source of bestiality."

If all we have to count on for the future is natural progress, education, and science, then all we can expect is the perpetual recurrence of what is and what has been, the truceless battle between light and darkness, the eternal conflict over the body of mankind, as Michael and the Devil disputed over the body of Moses. Is there any evidence that science, even should it conquer those great scourges of man's body, heart disease and cancer, will ever stop men from dying? Will progress ever stop men from sinning? Can knowledge ever wipe away all tears from our eyes or heal the broken heart? To ask these questions is to answer them.

Others hold that the great end—the triumph of righteousness and peace—will come, not through any natural law of progress and evolution, but through the expansion and development of the spiritual forces which are now at work in the world through the church. The world, they remind us, is bad enough with Christianity. What would it be without it? Think of the changes which have been enacted. Think of the progress that has been made. Think of the promises that are given. Did Christ not say that the kingdom of heaven "is like unto leaven, which a woman took, and hid in three measures of meal, till the whole was leavened" (Matt. 13:33)? Did He not say that the kingdom of heaven "is like to a grain of mustard seed, which a man took, and sowed in his field: which is indeed the least of all seeds: but when it is grown, it is the greatest among herbs, and becometh a tree, so that the birds of the air come and lodge in the branches thereof" (Matt. 13:31-32)?

Was not the vision given unto Ezekiel of the healing waters which issued from under the threshold of the holy house—first up to the ankles, then up to the knees, then up to the loins, then a river to swim in, a river that could not be passed, a river which brought life wherever it flowed and healed the waters of the Dead Sea? Do we not have there the picture of the gradual conquest of the world through the expansion of the spiritual forces now in the church? Do these not point to the day when "righteousness shall be the girdle of his loins and faithfulness the girdle of his reins.

The wolf also shall dwell with the lamb, and the leopard shall lie down with the kid; . . . and the sucking child shall play on the hole of the asp, and the weaned child shall put his hand on the cockatrice's den. They shall not hurt nor destroy in all my holy mountain: for the earth shall be full of the knowledge of the Lord, as the waters cover the sea" (Isa. 11:5-9)?

These are indeed great and beautiful promises, and a great encouragement to the church in its work. But there is more to reckon with than a gradual growth and spread of righteousness. Whatever those figures used by Christ mean, the opened heaven, the shaken earth, travail, anguish and woe, the sun turned into darkness and the moon into blood, certainly they do not indicate a slow, gradual ripening into perfection. In that same address and among those other parables of the Kingdom, like the mustard seed and the leaven in the measures of meal, there is the brief but profound parable of the wheat and the tares. When the servants of the householder asked permission to pull up the tares, he said, "Let them both grow together until the harvest" (Matt. 13:30). This tells us that there is a growth and development of evil as well as good. The wheat and the tares grow side by side unto the harvest. Neither wheat nor tares can harvest themselves. Our Lord, after He encouraged men to pray by the parable of the unjust judge, and gave assurance that God will avenge His own elect, asked that solemn question, with the implied negative answer, "When the Son of man cometh, shall he find faith on the earth?"

No, the final victory will come, not through natural progress, not through the expansion of the religious forces now at work in the world, but through another mighty act of God. Whatever the intermediate steps may be, whatever the ebb and flow of progress, the end will come, not by the improvement or the development of the present order, but through the complete supercession of it. The climax of history will be the appearance on the field of battle of the captain of our salvation Himself, and the glory of it will be comparable to what John beheld—the white horse and his rider going forth conquering and to conquer, with many crowns upon his head.

When the army of Julian the Apostate was on the march to Persia, some of the soldiers were tormenting and torturing a Christian believer. Wearying at length of their brutal sport, they looked down on their helpless victim and asked him with infinite scorn, "Where now is your Carpenter-God?" The man looked up at them through his blood and tears and answered, "He is making a coffin for your emperor." Yes, for every God-defying person and power and principle, for all that exalts itself against God and His Word, the coffin is now preparing.

When Christ comes as conqueror, He will pronounce the divine doom upon all wicked civilization and all inhuman forms of cruelty and lust, and upon all the enemies of God and righteousness, not only partially and locally, as hitherto, just enough to show us that there is a God who judges, but universally, in the whole created world. Once He was despised and rejected of men; then every knee shall bow. Once men railed on Him with their tongue; then every tongue shall confess that Christ is Lord. Once He was dumb with silence; then His voice shall shake both the heavens and the earth. Once they put a crimson robe on Him and mocked Him; then He will wear the crimson vesture of His triumphant atonement. Once twelve humble men followed Him about; then the armies of heaven will follow in His train. Once they pressed a crown of thorns upon His brow; then He will wear many crowns upon His head.

Some time ago the train on which I was traveling stopped at Ashtabula, Ohio. At once my mind recalled the great railroad disaster of 1876, when a train went through the bridge there taking the lives of many people, among them the famous evangelist and singer and composer of hymns, P. P. Bliss. One of his best-known hymns is "Hold the Fort." After the fall of Atlanta, in July, 1864, General John B. Hood, the commander of the Confederate army, marched westward to attack the communications of Sherman with Chattanooga and Nashville, hoping to draw back Sherman's army from Georgia. One of the posts he attacked was Allatoona Pass, commanded by the brave and capable General Corse. Sherman himself went back with part of his army as far as Kenesaw Mountain, where a battle had been fought some months before. From the summit of the mountain he heliographed to the beleaguered garrison at Allatoona Pass, "Hold the fort! I am coming!"

In Sherman's army at the time was a Major Whittle, afterward a well-known evangelist. Whittle related the incident to Bliss, who, taking it for his inspiration, wrote the hymn:

"Hold the fort, for I am coming,"
  Jesus signals still;
Wave the answer back to heaven,
  "By thy grace we will."

The message of Christ to His church is "Occupy till I come!" He may come at the midnight watch. He may come in the third watch. He may come in the fourth watch, as He came that night walking over the waves to the disciples in the storm-driven ship on Galilee's Sea. But whatever hour He comes, "Blessed are those servants, whom the Lord when he cometh shall find watching: verily I say unto you, that he shall gird himself, and make them to sit down to meat, and will come forth and serve them" (Luke 12:37). What a day that will be! Then none shall be sorry that he fought the good fight and finished the course and kept the faith.

Lift up your hearts! Our King shall come! Our cause shall conquer! When the world sky is darkest with clouds of unbelief, behold the glory of the Coming of the Lord. Above all the chariots and horsemen of this world, behold the white horse and his rider; and when the babel sounds are loudest in their scornful derision of God and His eternal Son, you shall hear floating down from heaven the notes of that distant triumph song whose sweet melody shall one day encompass the heavens and the earth, "Alleluia: for the Lord God omnipotent reigneth!" (Rev. 19:6). "The kingdoms of this world are become the kingdoms of our Lord, and of his Christ; and he shall reign forever and ever" (Rev. 22:5).

18

ALPHA AND OMEGA

I am Alpha and Omega, the beginning and the end (Revelation 21:6).

The Bible begins at the beginning and ends at the end. It is the only book which tells us about the beginning and also about the end. It alone has the conception of a great movement towards righteousness, ever growing, ever increasing, until it reaches its magnificent climax in the Kingdom of God. The book of Revelation declares and exhibits the glory of that climax.

No book has been so abused, and also so neglected, as the book of Revelation. It has been a favorite camping ground for those who write history before it has been enacted. At the other extreme, it has suffered from total neglect. Yet the book is the necessary supplement to all else in the Bible. It is here that we behold the triumph of those truths and principles which are taught in the rest of the New Testament.

We ourselves see too much, and at the same time too little; and what we do see appears to be opposed to, and stronger than, what we believe. But here in the book of Revelation, where the whole panorama of God's battle with evil unfolds itself, we behold the vision of the conquering Redeemer. Christ, the Man of Sorrows, is transformed into the King of Kings and the Lord of Lords, and beyond and above and around the death-stricken order of this world stretches His everlasting Kingdom.

In this text—"I am Alpha and Omega, the beginning and the end"—we have one of the tremendous utterances of the book of

Revelation. It is spoken at the beginning of the revelations con-
tained in the book, and again at the end, when the drama of human
history and of the conflict of the church with the world has been
finished. For his testimony to Christ, John had been banished to the
Isle of Patmos, some sixty or seventy miles off the coast of Asia
Minor. He had not gone there as some, although always very few,
go to that remote island today, to enjoy the beauty of it, or to let the
mind expatiate in its grand memories. He was there as a prisoner of
Christ. Possibly it was in the reign of the Emperor Domitian, possibly in the reign of the brutal Emperor Nero. But John had not
forgotten the Christian calendar, and he "was in the Spirit on the
Lord's day" (Rev. 1:10). As he prayed and meditated he heard behind him a great voice as of a trumpet, and, turning about, saw one
like unto the Son of man standing in the midst of the seven golden
candlesticks. "His head and His hairs were white like wool, as white
as snow; and His eyes were as a flame of fire" (Rev. 1:15). His feet
burned like a furnace and His voice was as the sound of many
waters. In his right hand He held the seven stars and out of His
mouth went a sharp, two-edged sword, and His countenance was as
the sun shineth in his strength (see Rev. 1:15, 16).

Overcome by this awful presence, John fell at His feet as one
dead. But the glorious person laid His hand upon him, saying
unto him: "Fear not; I am the first and the last. I am he that liveth,
and was dead; and, behold, I am alive for evermore, Amen; and
have the keys of hell and of death. Write the things which thou
hast seen, and the things which are, and the things which shall be
hereafter" (Rev. 1:17-19).

Those things which John saw, the things which are, and the
things which shall be hereafter, make up the book of Revelation.
All that transpires there is by virtue of the authority of him who is
Alpha and Omega, the beginning and the end. When at length all
those things have come to pass, when the Lamb has opened the
seven-sealed book of mystery, when the seven seals have been
opened, and the seven angels have sounded, and all the judgments
have been pronounced, and the last great battle has been fought,
and the Babylon of evil has fallen, and Satan has been overthrown
and judged, and death and hell have been cast into the lake of fire,
and the new heaven and the new earth have come, and the holy
city, new Jerusalem, has come down from God out of heaven, and

all things are made new, then again He who spoke to John on the Isle of Patmos speaks now from the throne of a redeemed universe, saying, "It is done. I am Alpha and Omega."

CHRIST IS THE ALPHA AND OMEGA OF THE SCRIPTURES

Alpha and omega are the first and last letters of the Greek alphabet. The history of the alphabet, these signs which represent sounds and accents of speech, is a very curious one. The origin of the alphabet is wrapped in the mists of mystery which envelop the early history of mankind. At first the alphabet seems to have been a series of pictures, representing not only words and sounds, but ideas.

For us today the alphabet is a series of signs which represent sounds, and the combination of letters, words. Today those signs or letters have no connection at all with this original use. But as it now stands, those signs and letters are the mode of expression, the vehicle of thought. All that man can say to man, all his knowledge of the past, all his skill in the present, all his hope and aspiration for the future, is summed up in words made up of the letters of the alphabet. When we say then that Christ is Alpha and Omega, the first and the last letter of the alphabet, we say that in Him is summed up all of the divine thought and revelation for man.

From the very beginning the church adopted alpha and omega as one of its favorite and most impressive symbols. It is worked into the architecture of churches, wrought into the stained glass of cathedral windows, engraved on Bible markers, and inscribed on the graves of the Christian dead. Like all great utterances of Christ, and like all great symbols, it expresses far more than our human minds can know or utter. That is the very appeal of it, that it expresses for us all the power and majesty, the redeeming love, and the eternal Kingdom of Christ.

Christ is the Alpha and the Omega of the Bible. What is the Bible? One might answer that it is a collection of sixty-six books, written by thirty and more authors, through a millennium and a half of time, some of the authors highly educated men, others herdmen, tax gatherers, and fishermen. In the sixty-six books will be found almost every form of writing: historical narrative, prediction, biography, soliloquies, odes, dramas, hymns, proverbs, and codes of law.

But that is no answer to the question, What is the Bible? The best definition of the Bible is Christ's definition of it, "They are they which testify of me" (John 5:39). Christ stands in the midst of the Bible as John saw Him standing in the midst of the seven golden candlesticks. He is the eternal Word to whom the written word bears witness. In the Old Testament we listen to the predictions of His coming, the promise of a redeemer and a deliverer, His line of descent through Abraham, Isaac, Jacob, and David, His persecution, rejection, loneliness, betrayal, denial, suffering, death, resurrection, and everlasting reign. And in the New Testament we have the fulfillment of those great predictions. There we have the story of His birth and incarnation, His baptism, His temptation, His preaching, His miracles, His denial, His betrayal, His crucifixion, His death, His resurrection, His ascension into heaven, His outpouring of the Holy Spirit, and there too the promise of His coming again in glory. As a beautiful mosaic is made up of a thousand fragments of colored stones or glass, so out of all the chapters and books and verses of the Bible we have the face of Christ, the Son of God, the Savior of the world. There we can say with William Cowper:

> My soul rejoices to pursue
> The steps of Him I love,
> Till glory breaks upon my view
> In brighter worlds above.

Without Christ the Bible is like a great cathedral wrapped in gloom and darkness, but with Christ, as the Alpha and Omega, it is like a great cathedral when the light of the morning sun brings out all the splendor of its massive walls, nave, choir, transept, roof, soaring arches, and its windows flaming with the faces of the goodly fellowship of the prophets, the glorious company of the apostles, and the noble army of the martyrs. When you take up the Bible to read, read it with the faith and realization that this is the Book of which Christ is the Alpha and the Omega, the beginning and the end, and that in its pages He speaks to your soul.

CHRIST IS THE ALPHA AND OMEGA OF THE CHURCH

When John heard Christ say, "I am Alpha and Omega," he saw Him standing in the midst of the seven golden candlesticks, which are the seven churches, and the seven stars which He held in His right hand are the angels or ministers of the churches. What is expressed there, then, is the Christ as the light and power and glory of His church.

Christ loved the individual soul. He loved the sinner. He loved the whole world. But He also loved the church and gave Himself for it. Here and there you hear of men who say they are interested in religion, admire Christ, perhaps even love and worship Him, but have no love for the church. That is false religion. They who do not love the church and would separate from it, must separate themselves from Christ, for nothing could be plainer than that Christ loved the church. He founded it upon the rock of His complete deity. He called its first apostles and gave them the everlasting gospel to proclaim. He gave the church its sacraments, assured it of His everlasting presence with it, of His never-to-be-withdrawn love for it, and of its final and glorious victory, a glory compared with which the brightest day that has yet dawned upon the world is darkness, and the fairest splendors which have invested it but the shadow of midnight.

The great business of the church is to exalt Christ, who said, "I, if I be lifted up from the earth, will draw all men unto me" (John 12:32). When we hear of churches where in the whole service there is no mention of Christ save in the benediction, we know that there is something wrong. The church is not here to exalt human wisdom or to propose human solutions. It is here to exalt Christ who is the Alpha and Omega. That is the reason the church has endured through the ages. The masonry of Rome's aqueducts and colosseums and arches has survived the empire itself, but the church of Christ is praying yet, a thousand years the same.

CHRIST IS THE ALPHA AND OMEGA OF TIME AND HISTORY

We speak of "Before Christ" and "After Christ"; but literally there is no before and after Christ, because He is before all things and He is after all things, the Alpha and Omega, the beginning and the end. History is but a parenthesis between two great utterances of God's Word, the first sentence of the Bible, "In the beginning God. . ." and this sentence, spoken at the end of human history, "It is done. I am Alpha and Omega."

The voice said to John on Patmos, "I am Alpha and Omega, the first and the last, [and I] have the keys of hell and of death." The keys are the symbol of authority and knowledge. Who but Christ holds the keys of world history and world movements? A bewildered humanity, perplexed and confused, and knowing not which way to turn, can look to no human personality who has the keys.

Certainly our politicians and statesmen do not have the keys. They are men of like passions with ourselves. What could be more apparent than that no system of government or of international government can solve the problem of mankind and bring lasting justice and peace on the earth? About all the statesmen of the present day can do is to attempt to unlock tomorrow's portal with the broken key of yesterday. Science does not have the key. Science blesses with one hand and smites with the other. Today the world waits and trembles to see what new horrors the inventive genius of man in the field of science can loose upon the world, what new and terrible Frankenstein the mind of man will devise and the hand of man will build for his misery and destruction.

Education does not have the key. We have invested the revenues of empires in our system of education. We have built colleges on every high hill and schoolhouses under every green tree. But who will say that they are able to cope with the moral problem of mankind?

Statesman, philosopher, educator, scientist—none holds the key. Only Christ holds the key. One of the paintings of the flight into Egypt shows the holy family at the Sphinx. The grim colossus is gazing out over the desert with that fixed, inscrutable look. Yonder Joseph sleeps on the sand under his robe. But the mother rests on the knees of the Sphinx, and in her arms sleeps the Holy Child. The artist evidently meant to portray the idea that Christ alone has the power and authority to solve the problem of human life, to answer its riddle, to illuminate its mystery.

Christ, as Alpha and Omega, presides over the movements of history. However terrible and unfortunate these movements are, we have the assurance that Christ is on His throne, that He is not a mere spectator, that the ages belong to Him, that all things, even in the darkest hour, proceed under His authority, and that above all world figures and world actors, is the great actor, Christ Himself, and that one day He who cried out of the darkness of Calvary,

"It is finished," shall cry again from the throne of a redeemed universe, "It is done. I am Alpha and Omega."

CONCLUSION

Christ is the Alpha and Omega of the believer. He is the Author and the Finisher of our faith. His Word is our rule and law, His life our example and pattern, His death on the cross our salvation, His presence our joy, His smile our reward, to be with Him in glory everlasting, our eternal hope.

What place does Christ take in your life? To what degree can you and I say, "He is for me the Alpha and the Omega, the first and the last, the beginning and the end"? He who is the Lord of the ages, the King of time, and the adored of the angels, is worthy of the first place in your life and heart. Will you give that place to Him? No one ever did that and lived to regret it. On the contrary, you will be able to say, as Frances Ridley Havergal wrote:

> Jesus, Master, whose I am,
>   Purchased Thine alone to be,
> By Thy blood, O spotless Lamb,
>   Shed so willingly for me;
> Let my heart be all Thine own,
> Let me live to Thee alone.
>
> Other lords have long held sway;
>   Now, Thy name alone to bear,
> Thy dear voice alone obey,
>   Is my daily, hourly prayer.
> Whom have I in heaven but Thee?
> Nothing else my joy can be.
>
> Jesus, Master! I am Thine;
>   Keep me faithful, keep me near,
> Let Thy presence in me shine
>   All my homeward way to cheer.
> Jesus! at Thy feet I fall,
> Oh, be Thou my All-in-all.